let not
your heart
be
troubled

let not your heart be troubled

40 Daily Meditations *on* Jesus *and* Prayer

HAROLD MYRA

Discovery House.
from Our Daily Bread Ministries

Discovery House is affiliated with Our Daily Bread
Ministries, Grand Rapids, Michigan.

Requests for permission to quote from this book should be directed
to: Permissions Department, Discovery House, PO Box 3566, Grand
Rapids, MI 49501, or contact us by email at permissionsdept@dhp.org.

Interior design by Sherri L. Hoffman

ISBN: 978-1-62707-919-8

Printed in the United States of America

First printing in 2019

Contents

Welcome 7

Consider . . . Jesus' Invitation 9

Part One: Praying Like Jesus

Day 1   Darkness and Light 13
Day 2   Fires of Sorrow 16
Day 3   The Source of Love 19
Day 4   The Delight Cycle 22
Day 5   Walk with Jesus 25
Day 6   Habits 28
Day 7   Keep Knocking 31
Day 8   Poor and Blessed 33
Day 9   Into the Thick of It 36
Day 10   Opening Our Eyes 39

Consider . . . Jesus' Stories about Prayer 42

Part Two: Our Heavenly Father

Day 11   Fatherless? 48
Day 12   Where Is God's Justice? 51
Day 13   Shaken by Holiness 54
Day 14   "Always Working" 57
Day 15   The Best Invitation 60
Day 16   The Music of Life 63
Day 17   Our True Nature 66
Day 18   Satan's Strategy 69
Day 19   What Is Peace? 72
Day 20   "Don't Be Afraid" 75

Consider . . . Jesus' Straight Talk about Prayer 78

Part Three: Our Troubled Times

Day 21   The Evil Commander 83
Day 22   "All Shall Be Well" 86
Day 23   When Someone Betrays You 89
Day 24   Is Joy Possible? 92
Day 25   Look for the Fun 95
Day 26   Prayer in Disaster 98
Day 27   Shouting into Silence 101
Day 28   In Heaven's Light 104
Day 29   Mortal, yet in God's Image 107
Day 30   Fly to Safety? 110

Consider . . . Jesus Praying 112

Part Four: Jesus in Trouble

Day 31   What's My Role? 117
Day 32   Prayer for Fellow Believers 120
Day 33   Joy and Hatred 122
Day 34   Holiness: Wholeness 125
Day 35   What Awes Us? 127
Day 36   The World Is Watching 129
Day 37   What Will We See? 132
Day 38   War in Heaven 134
Day 39   Resurrection Joy 137
Day 40   The Ultimate Answer to Prayer 140

Appendix: Prayer throughout the Scriptures 143

Notes 157

WELCOME

We see their faces on our screens: refugee children fearful and disoriented; survivors of violence grieving for loved ones; enraged women accusing men; distraught witnesses to a teenager's overdose or suicide. We know so much these days, and we see so much. We're torn by the suffering of so many, and we're anxious about threats of war and national collapse while a cacophony of angry voices blame "the other side."

How can we pray authentically in these troubled times?

We may be praising God for his grace and experiencing prayer as comfort and guidance . . . yet our prayers sometimes seem unanswered, like bottles with unread messages floating in the sea.

When we pray, can we sense our heavenly Father is actually listening and that we're in tune with his Holy Spirit?

Jesus presents the ultimate model. He provided for us a vibrant legacy of illustrations, teachings, and experiences. Prayer was central to his life.

Jesus was all about prayer because he was here on a mission from his heavenly Father. He stayed in constant communion with him.

The following prayer devotions explore what all that means to us as we navigate life in our dramatically changing times. We have a wealth of firsthand descriptions of Jesus' prayer life, his teachings and his stories about prayer. We'll meditate on his personal prayers and how his stories can shape ours, and we'll see how his teachings on prayer are resonant with the Scriptures he affirmed.

Jesus promised the Holy Spirit would be our guide as we respond to him.

This book is divided into four parts: Praying Like Jesus, Our Heavenly Father, Troubled Times, and Jesus in Trouble.

For each of the forty days, psalm-like prayers are interwoven with excerpts from one chapter of Scripture. The selected lines are relevant to the day's topic, and the lines are broken to help us focus afresh on what each line means. Each prayer devotion ends with a "Prayer for Today"—a sentence or two that we can remember and pray throughout the day to keep our hearts and minds fixed on our Sustainer.

In our troubled times, what better advice could we find than that of Philippians 4:6–7: "Don't worry about anything; instead, pray about everything. Tell God what you need, and thank him for all he has done. Then you will experience God's peace, which exceeds anything we can understand. His peace will guard your hearts and minds as you live in Christ Jesus."

Jesus' Invitation

MATTHEW 11:28—29; 7:7

Then Jesus said, "Come to me, all of you who are weary and carry heavy burdens, and I will give you rest. Take my yoke upon you. Let me teach you, because I am humble and gentle at heart, and you will find rest for your souls."

"Keep on asking, and you will receive what you ask for. Keep on seeking, and you will find. Keep on knocking, and the door will be opened to you."

ᥫᩤ

PART ONE

Praying Like Jesus

Although he lived in a world of injustice, corruption, and impending catastrophe, Jesus told his followers, "Don't be troubled or afraid."

How could he say that?

Jesus lived by prayer, and he invited his followers to do the same. He said he could do nothing without his heavenly Father, and he would spend entire nights in prayer. That's why, when he was soon to go back to his Father he could say, "I am leaving you with a gift—peace of mind and heart. And the peace I give is a gift the world cannot give."

How true! The world cannot give us peace. But Jesus promises his peace, and the reason is remarkable: we can commune with our Father in heaven as he did throughout his life on earth. The prayer Jesus taught us to pray begins, "Our Father," which draws our minds and hearts into the majesty and wonders of our Creator who loves us.

When we feel anxious and fearful, saturating our minds with the love and magnificence of God is a marvelous antidote.

Scripture tells us God loves us so much he sent his Son to redeem us, and Jesus said, "All who love me will do what I say. My Father will love them and we will come and make our home with each of them."

What a startling promise!

When we pray as Jesus taught us—when we commune with his Father—we can begin to understand his saying, "So don't be troubled or afraid."

Some of us have opened ourselves to God's love and experienced his grace, yet we still feel anxiety about our families and our troubled world. We now live with comforts and conveniences unimagined by previous generations, yet we also live with fears about conflicts and catastrophes all over the world. Every day we witness events that make us stare in disbelief. Newscasters refer to "global upheavals."

When so much is tragic, and when we are all so vulnerable, how can we experience Jesus' mind-stretching promises? When our safety is threatened, our loved ones troubled, and our culture corrupted, how are we to pray with faith and hope?

For the next ten days we'll look at "the light that came into the world." As we draw closer to the light, our prayers will more closely align with his will, and we'll more clearly see our hurting world through our heavenly Father's eyes.

Darkness and Light

During Christmas services someone often reads from Isaiah 9: "The people who walk in darkness will see a great light. For those who live in a land of deep darkness, a light will shine." After the reading, with lights dimmed, someone holds out in the darkness one flickering candle to light another. A third wick catches the flame, and another and another, until all in the congregation are together lighting the sanctuary with their candles.

Light in the darkness—we all long for it. Light is what brings clarity, feelings of safety and confidence, certainty.

Earth is a beautiful place, full of wonders, yet millions "live in deep darkness." Fear. Insecurity. Wickedness. The gospel is the good news that into the world's turmoil and tragedy a Babe was born—that God so loved the world he sent his Son to redeem it.

Psalm 136 begins, "Give thanks to the LORD, for he is good! His faithful love endures forever." The psalmist goes on to describe many of the wonderful things God does, each time affirming, "His faithful love endures forever."

The troubles of our world seem to sharply contradict that. Where is God's love in the midst of wars and threats of wars? His faithful love endures forever. We need not panic. His faithful love endures forever.

Into darkness and despair God sent a great light on that first Christmas . . .

The Glorious Invasion

SELECTIONS FROM JOHN 1

In the beginning the Word already existed.
The Word was with God,
and the Word was God . . .

He came into the very world he had created,
but the world didn't recognize him. . . .
But to all who believed him and accepted him,
he gave the right to become children of God . . . .

So the Word became human and made his home
among us.
He was full of unfailing love and faithfulness.
And we have seen his glory,
the glory of the Father's one and only Son.

Father in heaven, here I am. Please draw me to your light. Help me to sense your unfailing love and faithfulness, no matter what is happening around me or elsewhere in the world. Instead of confusions and dread clamoring for my attention, let your glory and your grace fill me.

Thank you for sending your Son.

I praise you for the magnificent reality that you share your love and glory with us as your children. Help me to live today as your child, sensitive to your Holy Spirit and ready to be part of your purposes in the world, ready to bring light to the darkness in any small way that I can.

From his abundance we have all received
one gracious blessing after another.

Yes, Father! Don't let me take for granted all the blessings we've received. It's so easy to complain about what we lack and to dwell on the unjust things that happen to us . . . and the bad things that might happen. Thank you, Lord, for all your gracious blessings.

And thank you for your assurance that you love us.

All praise to you, Father in heaven, for the confident hope that your love for the world—the love that prompted you to send your Son—will ultimately change everything.

⌒

A PRAYER FOR TODAY

Draw me into your light all
through this day, Lord.
Fill me with praise and
gratitude for your love.

DAY 2

Fires of Sorrow

More than a hundred years ago Oswald Chambers declared, "Sorrow is one of the biggest facts in life." Despite human "progress," that hasn't changed. Even in relative safety and prosperity, we experience pain and personal loss. Chambers advised us to get realistic about sorrow, accepting it as part of life.

In our age of constant change and heated racial, gender, and religious conflicts, many find their sense of identity uncertain. Chambers challenged his listeners to pray "that I may preserve the self God created me to be through every fire of sorrow."

God created each of us with unique DNA, in a specific time and place where we all experience struggles and sorrow. As we cry out to the Lord, we respond as the "self he created us to be," in harmony with Father, Son, and Spirit.

Described as "a man of sorrows, acquainted with deepest grief," Jesus was sure of his identity as the beloved Son of his Father. He spoke of our being like seeds that need to die in order to be fruitful.

Yet the paradox is, he was also the man of joy, for through his suffering came both his joy of returning to the Father and accomplishing our redemption and our joy of peace with God.

In the selections that follow we see the realism in his teaching, and we see in his prayer our Lord's firm resolve to complete his mission despite the suffering ahead.

When Jesus Was Troubled

SELECTIONS FROM JOHN 12

"I tell you the truth, unless a kernel of wheat
is planted in the soil and dies, it remains alone.
But its death will produce many new kernels—
a plentiful harvest of new lives.
Those who love their life in this world
> *will lose it. . . .*
The Father will honor anyone who serves me."

Lord Jesus, I want to serve you and to please your Father. I don't want to love my life more than I love you. Yet I'm painfully aware my love for you is weak. You once said some seeds fall on stony ground and others on good soil. Let mine be good soil, receptive to your seeds of love and grace.

Fill me with love for you, and help me to serve you and others.

"Now my soul is deeply troubled.
Should I pray, 'Father, save me from this hour'?
But this is the very reason I came!
Father, bring glory to your name."

Lord Jesus, sometimes I wonder how I'm to respond to sorrows that cut to the bone.

Sometimes I want to escape!

Sometimes I want to shake my head asking, "Why me?"

But you too faced "terrible sorrows," and you were "deeply troubled" by the dreadful things ahead of you, but you didn't pray to escape them. You were determined to fulfill your Father's purpose. Am I fulfilling your Father's purpose for me, even though I fail and feel overwhelmed?

Please cleanse my soul in this refining furnace.

"Walk in the light while you can,
so the darkness will not overtake you . . .
Put your trust in the light while there is still time;
then you will become children of the light."

Father in heaven, I want to be a child of the light. As I drag my concerns and baggage into your light, shine on me, Lord!

Yes, shine on me.

Cleanse me.

Clear my eyes so I see from your perspective.

⌒

A Prayer for Today

Whatever I face today, Lord,
help me to welcome your loving,
cleansing, energizing presence.

DAY 3

The Source of Love

"For God so loved the world . . ."

Does he really?

For skeptics, the apostle John's bold assertion in his gospel that God loves the world seems flatly contradicted by harsh realities. The old pop song "What the World Needs Now Is Love" has been sung by millions, yet bitterness and revenge keep squelching empathy and love.

And if you think that our day is worse than the apostle John's, do some reading on the Roman empire and the revenge-seeking brutality inherent in the conflict. So where did the beloved disciple of Jesus gain his conviction that God loved the world?

We get plenty of clues when we turn to John's accounts of what Jesus said to him and the other disciples. Shortly before he was betrayed and taken before Pilate, he strongly emphasized his Father's love, and he made it practical: "So now I am giving you a new commandment: Love each other. Just as I have loved you, you should love each other. Your love for one another will prove to the world that you are my disciples."

That's how they would stand out in their day. And that's how we will stand out in ours. Those in fellowship with the Father, Son, and Spirit are called to be known for their love.

The source of authentic love is God. Today's Scripture includes selections of the personal things Jesus said about love and how we can receive it.

———— "My Father Will Love Them" ————
Selections from John 14

"If you love me, obey my commandments.
And I will ask the Father,
and he will give you another Advocate,
who will never leave you.
He is the Holy Spirit . . ."

Lord Jesus Christ, it's painfully clear to me that I cannot create love. My love for you does not come from me but from you and your Father. I want to love you and open myself now to your love. Thank you for the promise of your Holy Spirit to be here with me and to pour your love into me.

Help me to empty myself of my self-centeredness. Help me to be fully open to your love and to share it in the ways your Spirit shows me throughout this day.

"Those who accept my commandments
and obey them
are the ones who love me.
And because they love me,
my Father will love them.
And I will love them
and reveal myself to each of them."

Lord, show me how to obey your commands, for I know they're embedded in your love for me, in your love for all of us. Help me to reject cynicism and fear and bitterness.

"All who love me will do what I say.
My Father will love them,
and we will come
and make our home with each of them."

Thank you, Jesus, for this wonderful promise that you and your Father love me. Thank you for giving me the hope that today I can walk in your love because I am God's beloved child.

⁓

A PRAYER FOR TODAY

Father in heaven, grant me joy
today as I absorb what it means that
you make your home with me.

DAY 4

The Delight Cycle

Joy. Delight. Love. The Scriptures tell us how we can experience them.

The dynamic is described in Psalm 37:4: "Take delight in the LORD, and he will give you your heart's desires." If we're delighted with God and what delights him, the desires of our hearts will be in line with what he desires for us. His delight becomes our delight.

Similarly, Jesus said that when we obey his commands and remain in his love, our prayers are granted and joy overflows. Reading the words of Jesus shows us not only how to pray but gives us the promise that our prayers—asking, listening, obeying, praising—generate delight and joy. It's the blessed cycle of love and faith that brings glory to the Father and joy to us.

To see how strongly the Bible accentuates this dynamic, meditate on Psalm 119. There the psalmist celebrates God's commands over and over again; he finds sustaining joy in them.

We are part of the action that counts in this troubled planet. What we should do becomes very practical when we obey Jesus' command: "Love each other the same way I have loved you."

Great Glory

SELECTIONS FROM JOHN 15

"But if you remain in me
and my words remain in you,
you may ask for anything you want,
and it will be granted.
When you produce much fruit,
you are my true disciples.
This brings great glory to my Father."

Lord, when I neglect your words and fail to remain in you, bring me back so that what I ask will produce fruit from you. Help me to bring glory to you instead of thinking so much about what others think of me.

"I have loved you even as the Father has loved me.
Remain in my love.
When you obey my commandments,
you remain in my love,
just as I obey my Father's commandments
and remain in his love."

I want to remain in your love, and I know that's only possible if you pour your love into me. Here are my thoughts, concerns, and desires . . .

Let me be fully open to your Spirit.

"I have told you these things
so that you with be filled with my joy.
Yes, your joy will overflow!
This is my commandment:
Love each other in the same way I have loved you."

You know, Lord, that I seldom feel joy, let alone joy that overflows. You know also that I don't love others as you love us. Pour into me your love, Lord, for you and for others who need me to forgive them and to love them.

⌒

A Prayer for Today

Lord, even in today's difficulties, help me to
overflow with joy as I love you and love others.

DAY 5

Walk with Jesus

After Jesus' resurrection, the disciples who walked with him on the road to Emmaus said their hearts felt strangely warm as they were with him. Jesus has that effect on people.

If we are walking with Jesus and praying to his Father, closely aligned, we will be praying as he prays. And—it's far beyond our comprehension—Scripture tells us that he is always praying for us, pleading for us.

There's a warm and simple folk song that is a prayer:

Just a closer walk with Thee,
Grant it, Jesus, is my plea.
Daily walking close to Thee,
Let it be, dear Lord, let it be.

As we walk, we bring our global concerns to him. We bring our anxieties and disappointments, in others and in ourselves. We acknowledge our limitations and needs in the same breath that we acknowledge his power and capability. The lyrics confess,

I am weak, but thou art strong.
Jesus, keep me from all wrong;
I'll be satisfied as long
as I walk, let me walk, close to Thee.

The disciples on the road with the resurrected Jesus were fully engaged in listening to what he was teaching them. We have the same opportunity.

The Risen Lord

SELECTIONS FROM LUKE 24

Then Jesus took them through the writings of Moses
and all the prophets,
explaining from all the Scriptures the things
concerning himself. . . .

As they sat down to eat, he took the bread and
blessed it.
Then he broke it and gave it to them.
Suddenly their eyes were opened,
and they recognized him.
And at that moment he disappeared!

They said to each other,
"Didn't our hearts burn within us
as he talked with us on the road
and explained the Scriptures to us?"

Help me, Lord, to recognize what you are teaching me. Grant me your power to understand what the Scriptures teach about you and how I should obey what applies to me.

Thank you for walking with me.

Within the hour they were on their way back
to Jerusalem.
There they found the eleven disciples
and the others who had gathered with them, who said,
"The Lord has really risen! He appeared to Peter."

Then the two from Emmaus told their story . . .
And just as they were telling about it,
Jesus himself was suddenly standing there among
them.
"Peace be with you," he said.

Lord, I long for your peace and the assurance that you really are walking with me through all that's before me now. Give us who follow you a sense of your presence and the joy that comes from your being "really risen"!

 ᡠᡠ

A PRAYER FOR TODAY

All through this day, Lord, let me walk
"close to thee" and find my satisfaction
in the realities of your resurrection.

DAY 6

Habits

Theologian Vernon Grounds contrasts typical habits that can become ruts with good spiritual habits that become "grooves of grace."

Recent research shows that despite our best intentions, our willpower to change our habits is much more limited than we might think. It also shows the most effective strategy for breaking bad ones is to replace them with good ones.

If you have a bad habit that needs replacing, try replacing it with prayer!

Jesus had a habit of spending time with his Father. We read in the first chapter of Mark, "Before daybreak the next morning, Jesus got up and went to an isolated place to pray." We find in the Gospels many such mentions of his prayer life.

Practicing the presence of God is a "groove of grace" that leads to fresh starts, builds habits that free us from old ruts, and prepares us for when the inevitable storms of life hit.

Many of us live busy lives and find it difficult to find time to commune with our heavenly Father. Yet prioritizing prayer allows both preparation for the stress to come and opportunity to release the stresses of the day into God's control. When Jesus saw a huge crowd waiting for him, he had compassion on them, taught them, fed them bread and fish, and sent them home. Then he told his disciples to go across the lake, and he went up into the hills to pray.

Alone In the Hills

Selections from Mark 6

The apostles returned to Jesus from their ministry
*   tour*
and told him all they had done and taught.
Then Jesus said, "Let's go off by ourselves
to a quiet place and rest awhile." . . .

Jesus insisted that his disciples get back into
*   the boat*
and head across the lake. . . .
He went up into the hills by himself to pray.

Lord, I want more and more to practice your presence and develop the habit of spending time with you in prayer. Help me to see how I can prioritize prayer while still getting done all that's before me each day.

Thank you for the invitation to come to you and to lay my burdens and requests before you.

Late that night, the disciples were in their boat
in the middle of the lake,
and Jesus was alone on land.
He saw that they were in serious trouble,
rowing hard and struggling against the wind
*   and waves. . . .*
Jesus came toward them, walking on the water. . . .
They cried out in terror, thinking he was a ghost. . . .

But Jesus spoke to them at once.
"Don't be afraid," he said.
"Take courage! I am here!"

"In serious trouble." So often that describes the circumstances of people I care about. "Serious trouble" seems to be everywhere these days.

Since you are here with us, help me not to be afraid. Grant me the courage your presence brings. Whether the struggles are mine or someone else's, Lord, grant us faith and glimpses of your amazing grace.

A Prayer for Today

Help me, Lord, in both my troubles
and my joys, to believe your promise,
"Take courage! I am here!"

Keep Knocking

Asked by one of his disciples to teach them to pray, Jesus taught them the Our Father, and then he went on to teach them more about prayer using two stories.

In the first, he described a man at midnight pleading for help from a reluctant friend. The friend doesn't want to be bothered and tells the man to go away. And yet, finally, the friend relents because of the man's persistence. He contrasted that with pleading for help from their heavenly Father. His point was that if a friend finally relents, won't our loving Father respond to our prayers? Jesus said, "Keep on asking, and you will receive."

In the next story he draws another contrast between the human response to need and his Father's response. Sinful, imperfect human fathers don't give their children something dangerous and deadly when they ask for food. So how much more can we expect from our holy, perfect heavenly Father, who is full of compassion, in answer to our prayers, especially when we ask for the Holy Spirit's guidance?

In these stories, Jesus emphasized persistence and trust when we come to his Father . . .

Everyone Who Seeks

SELECTIONS FROM LUKE 11

"And so I tell you, keep on asking,
and you will receive what you ask for.
Keep on seeking, and you will find.
Keep on knocking,
and the door will be opened to you."

Holy Spirit of God, please help me understand Jesus' promises that if we keep asking and seeking and knocking that we'll receive what we ask for. Sometimes our prayers are wonderfully answered but other times our hopes in answered prayers seem dashed. I know we must accept your will and see from your perspective. Guide my thoughts and enable me to keep seeking and to keep praying even when I cannot see how the door is opened to me.

"For everyone who asks, receives.
Everyone who seeks, finds.
And to everyone who knocks,
the door will be opened."

Lord, I accept your promise that my asking and seeking and knocking will somehow be answered. Flow into my mind and heart the faith and persistence that comes from you. Help me to demonstrate my trust in you so that others' faith can be strengthened too. Help me to pray in the ways that please you. Keep me in harmony with you as I bring my concerns and requests to you.

A PRAYER FOR TODAY

Father in heaven, I have many concerns
and requests, and I lay them all before you.
Please answer my knocking at your door.

DAY 8

Poor and Blessed

Jesus' Beatitudes from the Sermon on the Mount convey a wealth of insight into authentic prayer. Starting with, "God blesses those who are poor and realize their need for him," they put the first essential front and center. We must realize we need him!

We are most blessed when we grasp how greatly and how constantly we need his love and grace.

Eugene Peterson in *The Message* paraphrases that same verse, Matthew 5:3, this way: "You're blessed when you're at the end of your rope. With less of you there is more of God and his rule."

And why are those who mourn blessed? We all experience the grief of losing loved ones, and many attest to the ways it compelled them into God's comfort. Hardship and loss drives us to God.

All through the Beatitudes, Jesus' descriptions of the persons who are blessed reflect attitudes that put them in harmony with the Father:

Those who are humble and merciful.

Those who crave justice.

Those whose hearts are pure.

Those who work for peace.

True prayer will flow naturally from these spiritual conditions of humility, mercy, and purity.

Mourning and Humility

SELECTIONS FROM MATTHEW 5

One day as he saw the crowds gathering,
Jesus went up on the mountainside and sat
down.
His disciples gathered around him,
and he began to teach them.

"God blesses those who are poor and realize
their need for him,
for the Kingdom of Heaven is theirs."

As time passes I realize more and more how much I need you, Lord, and how poor my life is when I am not in step with your Spirit. Help me to realize my need for you each day, and bring your blessings on me as I seek you in all aspects of my life.

"God blesses those who mourn,
for they will be comforted.
God blesses those who are humble,
for they will inherit the whole earth.
God blesses those who hunger and thirst
for justice,
for they will be satisfied."

Lord, comfort me in my grief as I mourn lost loved ones, lost relationships, lost innocence, lost opportunities. Bless me as I humbly come before you and ask for your presence and guidance and forgiveness and provision daily. And give me a genuine hunger for the justice you desire on earth, that I might be satisfied that I am contributing to your will being done on earth.

❧

A PRAYER FOR TODAY

Lord, help me to be aware of my
need for you throughout this day.

DAY 9

Into the Thick of It

As never before, we are globally aware of injustice, the horrors of warfare, and the countless ways evil crushes people's hopes. As we continue to meditate on Jesus' Beatitudes, we see how they show his full awareness of the human condition. Those who are blessed, he said, are not only humble and know their need for God but they also care about the suffering around them.

In the Beatitudes we see God's view of those who not only care about those in need of justice and mercy but do something for them, even when it's personally costly. Jesus says we will be blessed when we do what is right—attitudes of humility, pursuit of justice, acts of mercy, stand for purity, work for peace—and are maligned and persecuted for it.

We prefer, of course, to have our blessings come in less painful ways! Yet the Beatitudes make it clear that rich blessings come out of loss, pain, and striving. In our fallen world, sharing God's good news of redemption and his concerns for the poor and oppressed can generate resentments and enmity. Jesus is realistic that our prayers don't make everything sweetness and light . . . but our humble prayers and actions will ultimately be rewarded.

Peace and Persecution

SELECTIONS FROM MATTHEW 5

"God blesses those who are merciful,
  for they will be shown mercy.
God blesses those whose hearts are pure,
  for they will see God.
God blesses those who work for peace,
  for they will be called the children of God."

I want to have a pure heart as your child, yet it's hard to see how I can work for peace when so much is so confusing. Help me to see you and your purposes as I move through my day. Lord, help me to be a peacemaker, and help me to be wise about how I work for peace. Grant me a full measure of your Holy Spirit, and lead me to show mercy in the ways you will lead. Thank you for your mercy toward me every day.

"God blesses those who are persecuted for doing right,
  for the Kingdom of Heaven is theirs.

"God blesses you when people mock you
and persecute you and lie about you
and say all sorts of evil things against you
because you are my followers.
Be happy about it! Be very glad!
For a great reward awaits you in heaven."

Father in heaven, help me first to do right—show me the right ways. Yet even when my conscience is clear and I feel I am in step with you, it's a very hard stretch for me to be glad when people say evil things about me. As I try to authentically serve you, help me to receive your assurance and grace that you are "in my corner" and that you do reward those who do right.

⌒

A Prayer for Today

All through this day, Lord, give
me clear vision of how I can serve
you by doing what is right.

Opening Our Eyes

Jesus said that "your eye is like a lamp that provides light for your body." It's intriguing to consider that analogy for our day, in relation to our multiple devices and screens. He told his followers, "When your eye is healthy, your whole body is filled with light."

How can we have healthy eyes and our bodies be full of light?

We hear much nowadays about what happens when our eyes are locked on smartphones, described by many as "seductive devices." We're told they are creating an epidemic of addiction, anxiety, and depression. As our eyes keep flicking on them, marriages and other relationships suffer. And we grow more anxious.

We're all affected to some degree. We live in a wired world. What's the answer to this newest source of anxiety?

Opening our eyes to the wonders of God's creation—and the wonders of his love for us—changes the chemistry of body and soul. Praise is an antidote to our anxieties.

Jesus often quoted the psalms, which are full of praise. Turning our minds and our eyes to praising God is in some ways like changing the channel . . . or putting our phones aside. We praise God for his magnificent creation, and we praise him for our magnificent redemption through his Son.

Christians have long prayed the psalms, making the psalmist's words personal and lifting them to the Father in both joy and desperation. The following selections lift us and spark candid prayer about our human condition.

Night Sky and Planet Earth

SELECTIONS FROM PSALM 8

*O LORD, our Lord, your majestic name fills the
     earth!
   Your glory is higher than the heavens. . . .*

*When I look at the night sky and see the work of
     your fingers—
   the moon and the stars you set in place—
what are mere mortals that you should think about
     them,
   human beings that you should care for them?
Yet you made them only a little lower than God
   and crowned them with glory and honor.*

Father in heaven, I do praise your name. Help me glimpse your glory and majesty as creator of all I can see and touch and hear and taste. Thank you for the splendor of wildlife everywhere on the planet! Thank you for strawberries and sand and Saturn's rings and the northern lights and the laughter of children! Your wonders are beyond description.

Praise to you for your endless creativity. As we are made in your image, praise to you for letting us create. Thank you for orchestras and sculptures and poetry and all the stuff of life's vitality. We praise you for your wonderful works and allowing us to be part of them.

What are mere mortals indeed, that you care for us and give us such sobering responsibilities?

You gave them charge of everything you made,
putting all things under their authority—
the flocks and the herds
and all the wild animals,
the birds in the sky, the fish in the sea,
and everything that swims the ocean currents.

Lord, it's a wonder you have given us such power, yet what a mess we've made. And we keep at it. Our powers enable us to wreck so much of your creation, and our hearts harden against those we should love.

Have mercy on me, Father. Forgive my sins, and lead me into ways that honor you and bring about your kingdom on earth as it is in heaven.

Grant me wisdom, grace, and resilience.

༄

A PRAYER FOR TODAY

Open my eyes, Lord, to your wonderful
works, and open my ears to the
whispers of your Holy Spirit.

Jesus' Stories about Prayer

In many ways all Jesus' stories are about prayer, for they illustrated how to live in communion with his Father—or what happens when people don't. He was harshly critical of religious leaders, not because they obeyed their religious rules but because the rules trumped authentic prayers of humility and love as described in his Beatitudes.

In Luke's gospel, two of Jesus' stories illustrate his concerns: the unjust judge contrasted with the heavenly Father, and the humble tax collector contrasted with a hypocritical religious leader. Jesus presents authentic prayer as persistent, humble, and childlike.

LUKE 18:1–17 NIV

The Parable of the Persistent Widow

Then Jesus told his disciples a parable to show them that they should always pray and not give up. He said: "In a certain town there was a judge who neither feared God nor cared what people thought. And there was a widow in that town who kept coming to him with the plea, 'Grant me justice against my adversary.'

"For some time he refused. But finally he said to himself, 'Even though I don't fear God or care what people think, yet because this widow keeps bothering me, I will see that she gets justice, so that she won't eventually come and attack me!'"

And the Lord said, "Listen to what the unjust judge says. And will not God bring about justice for his chosen ones, who cry out to him day and night?

Will he keep putting them off? I tell you, he will see that they get justice, and quickly. However, when the Son of Man comes, will he find faith on the earth?"

The Parable of the Pharisee and the Tax Collector

To some who were confident of their own righteousness and looked down on everyone else, Jesus told this parable: "Two men went up to the temple to pray, one a Pharisee and the other a tax collector. The Pharisee stood by himself and prayed: 'God, I thank you that I am not like other people—robbers, evildoers, adulterers—or even like this tax collector. I fast twice a week and give a tenth of all I get.'

"But the tax collector stood at a distance. He would not even look up to heaven, but beat his breast and said, 'God, have mercy on me, a sinner.'

"I tell you that this man, rather than the other, went home justified before God. For all those who exalt themselves will be humbled, and those who humble themselves will be exalted."

The Little Children and Jesus

People were also bringing babies to Jesus for him to place his hands on them. When the disciples saw this, they rebuked them. But Jesus called the children to him and said, "Let the little children come to me, and do not hinder them, for the kingdom of God belongs to such as these. Truly I tell you, anyone who will not receive the kingdom of God like a little child will never enter it."

PART TWO

Our Heavenly Father

Every day, Christians all over the world join other believers in saying the prayer Jesus taught his disciples. We might well feel both wonder and gratitude for his extraordinary invitation to commune directly with his heavenly Father.

Since Jesus said he could do nothing without his Father, what about us?

Jesus provides a model for approaching the Father that is succinct, yet complete.

The disciples knew Jesus' prayer life was central to all he said and did, and they were aware of his intense love for his Father, so it was natural they would ask him to teach them to pray. The model he shared with them was succinct, yet theologians have always marveled at its completeness. Consider the familiar words derived from Matthew 6:9–13:

> Our Father in heaven,
> holy be your name,
> your kingdom come,

your will be done,
on earth as it is in heaven.
Give us today our daily bread.
And forgive us our sins,
as we forgive those who sin against us.
And lead us not into temptation,
but deliver us from evil.

Jesus starts by focusing on the first essential. Instead of rushing into our requests and pleading for what we want God to do, we first recognize we have a Father in heaven.

Those of us blessed with a loving relationship with an earthly father know how empowering and marvelous that is. The fact we can have a loving relationship with our heavenly Father is a revelation full of promise and hope. Jesus tells us we have a Father we can call on, a Father who listens to his children. The prayer Jesus taught acknowledges our heavenly Father is holy, and that God has a purpose for us on earth that resonates with his purposes in heaven.

The psalmists often urge us to sing and even shout our praises to the Lord. To genuinely praise him, we need to know of "his wonderful works," and there is none more wonderful than his so loving the world that he sent his only Son to redeem us. God is holy, not in the caricatured way TV and movies depict "holier-than-thou" characters, but holiness as wholeness and health and purity and joy.

We pray, "Your will be done, on earth as it is in heaven" because our heavenly Father's will transforms and redeems his creation. We pray for breakthroughs of his heavenly will, breakthroughs of redemption and grace on earth.

In this model of prayer, only after we affirm our Father and his heavenly works do we bring him our requests. In fact, that's the briefest part of the prayer, one line only. Then we get down to dealing with our weaknesses and sins, asking for our Father's forgiveness as we forgive those who sin against us. Elsewhere Jesus firmly said we must forgive others if we expect to be forgiven ourselves.

And then we pray about our temptations and about the Evil One. There is no hiding from the fact we are tempted and that evil is rampant in the world. We bring that to our Father with a call for his engagement, for his power to be shown, and for our empowerment by his holiness—"deliver us from the evil one" (NIV).

So Jesus, in describing how to pray, shows us that first we call to the fatherly, holy God revealed in the Scriptures. We affirm his justice and his purposes on earth. Then we make requests and ask for his cleansing and grace—and for protection against the evil powers so evidently active everywhere.

DAY 11

Fatherless?

If you've seen the statistics on children without fathers, you know they're painful to look at. In our collapsing culture of broken families and disengaged men, the impact on children includes a long, blunt list of realities, among them high rates of suicide, homelessness, and runaway children. The well-respected book *Fatherless America* identifies fatherlessness as our greatest social problem.

In many ways the dysfunctions of the larger human "family" are essentially fatherlessness. Theologians sometimes describe our plight in today's world as being like children lost in a dark, menacing forest . . . children with no one to guide and protect.

Our world can seem fatherless indeed.

Yet Jesus emphasized we are *not* fatherless. He strongly asserted we have a heavenly Father who knows every hair on our heads. Most remarkable of all, Jesus emphasized we have a Father who knows us and loves us.

That's far from obvious, considering what we experience and see around us! Yet Jesus invites us to bring our dismay and our longings and our fears to this Father who loves us . . . and to welcome his Holy Spirit into our hearts and minds.

—— Our Father's Love ——

SELECTIONS FROM JOHN 16

"The Father himself loves you dearly
because you love me and believe that I came
*   from God.*
Yes, I came from the Father into the world,
And now I will leave the world and return to
*   the Father."*

Lord Jesus, I believe my heavenly Father loves me dearly; please help my unbelief. Clear away my guilt, doubts, and fears.

Help me to trust and obey.

What a wonder that you came from the Father and now are with him and still care about us. Give me eyes to see and a heart that beats in rhythm with your vitality.

Help me to love you, Lord.

"Do you finally believe?
But the time is coming . . .
when you will be scattered. . . .
I have told you all this
so that you may have peace in me.
Here on earth you will have many trials
*   and sorrows.*
But take heart, because I have overcome
*   the world."*

We long for your peace in our trials and sorrows that seem unending. Grant me your resilience and faith. Give me a taste of your triumph over evil and suffering. And thank you for your great sacrifices on my behalf.

Pour into my heart and mind gratitude and joy.

⁓

A Prayer for Today

Our Father in heaven, holy be your name.
I praise you for your love.

DAY 12

Where Is God's Justice?

When day after day we see so many human tragedies—from terrorism to tsunamis—we wonder: If our heavenly Father loves us, and if God is almighty and could change everything, why doesn't he?

Does our Father really care about our troubles?

We read in Luke 4 that after Jesus was tempted by Satan in the wilderness, he was filled with the Holy Spirit's power. In the village of Nazareth, his boyhood home, he went on the Sabbath to the synagogue and stood to read the Scriptures. "The Spirit of the LORD is upon me," he read from Isaiah 61, "for he has anointed me to bring Good News to the poor." He continued reading the prophecy that proclaimed release for captives, sight for the blind, and freedom for the oppressed.

After reading the passage Jesus said, "The Scripture you've just heard has been fulfilled this very day!"

Jesus' ministry of healing, spiritual cleansing, and confronting injustice described by Isaiah centuries before demonstrated God's compassion. "For I, the LORD, love justice," the prophecy declares. "I hate robbery and wrongdoing." And what will God do about it? "The Sovereign LORD will show his justice to the nations of the world. Everyone will praise him!"

Justice is coming. God so loved the world he sent his Son.

We read in 1 John 4:8, "God is love." Jesus came to show the depths and redemptive initiatives of his love.

Good News

SELECTIONS FROM ISAIAH 61

The Spirit of the Sovereign LORD is upon me,
for the LORD has anointed me
to bring good news to the poor.
He has sent me to comfort the brokenhearted
and to proclaim that captives will be released
and prisoners will be freed.
He has sent me to tell those who mourn
that the time of the LORD's favor has come.

Thank you, Lord, for your compassion for those with broken hearts and broken lives. There are so many prisoners and victims of atrocities and injustices! Help me to be part of what you are doing to share your compassion and mercies. Fill me with faith in your ultimate justice for the nations and for those who suffer.

To all who mourn in Israel,
he will give a crown of beauty for ashes,
a joyous blessing instead of mourning,
festive praise instead of despair.
In their righteousness, they will be like great oaks
that the LORD has planted for his own glory.

Father in heaven, what a wonderful vision that those who mourn will truly be comforted! And not only will they be comforted— they will know you and be full of beauty and strength and praise.

I am overwhelmed with joy in the LORD my God!
For he has dressed me with the clothing of
salvation
and draped me in a robe of righteousness.

I'm trying to understand, Lord, this image of putting on clothes that come from you. I want to be clothed by you. Put on me your clothing of grace and righteousness.

Thank you for your redeeming love for me, and for all who call on you and welcome you into their lives.

⟳

A PRAYER FOR TODAY

I trust in your justice, Father. Your
kingdom come, your will be done,
on earth as it is in heaven.

DAY 13

Shaken by Holiness

When Isaiah saw the Lord glorious in his temple, with winged creatures crying "holy, holy, holy is the Lord," he was shaken to the core. "I am doomed," he said, "for I am a sinful man. I have filthy lips, and I live among a people with filthy lips."

Considering the degradation of our culture and what we see and hear on our screens as "entertainment," we might well respond like Isaiah if brought into our heavenly Father's presence. Considering our own sins, we, too—confronted with his grandeur and holiness—would be shaken.

Jesus came to earth from such grandeur and holiness.

He was sinless.

How, then, can we come to his holy Father as he did?

"Your sins are forgiven," Jesus said as he healed a man. Isaiah, full of guilt and shattered by his glimpse of God's holiness, was cleansed, healed, forgiven . . . and given work to do. We, too, are cleansed and reconciled when we confess our sins and receive God's redemption.

We can pray like Jesus because he stands in our place before his Father, interceding for us, the recipients of his gift of eternal life.

The Burning Coal

SELECTIONS FROM ISAIAH 6

It was in the year King Uzziah died that I saw the Lord.
He was sitting on a lofty throne . . .
Attending him were mighty seraphim . . .
They were calling out to each other,

"Holy, holy, holy is the LORD of Heaven's Armies!
The whole earth is filled with his glory!"

Lord, when at Christmas I join people singing Handel's *Messiah,* and when I hear a choir singing "Amazing Grace," I get a glimpse of your glory. Thank you for the wonder of such glimpses and moments in prayer when I sense your grace.

I said, "It's all over!
I am doomed, for I am a sinful man.
I have filthy lips,
And I live among a people of filthy lips."

How true this is, Lord, of the culture I dwell in and what goes through my mind even when I am seeking to live in step with your Spirit. Have mercy on me.

Then one of the seraphim flew to me
with a burning coal he had taken from the altar. . . .
He touched my lips with it and said, . . .
"Now your guilt is removed, and your sins are forgiven."

Then I heard the Lord asking,
"Whom should I send as a messenger to this people?
Who will go for us?"

I said, "Here I am. Send me."

I know cleansing comes only from you and that your holy angels are here to help me. Forgive my sins, and show me how I should contribute to conveying your messages and grace to this troubled world . . . and to those around me struggling to live for you in our cultural chaos.

∽

A Prayer for Today

Give us this day our daily bread, and
forgive us our sins, as we forgive
those who sin against us.

DAY 14

"Always Working"

Jesus said he and his Father "are always working." Now that's a reality worth savoring!

The fact Jesus and his Father are always working together and inviting us to join them is rather stunning. Our world may seem out of control, like Father, Son, and Holy Spirit are absent. Yet Jesus declared they are always at work.

"God is up to something." Preachers have used that phrase to declare the Spirit's work in creation and in our lives. We may not see or understand what's going on in his fresh creativities and acts of redemption, but Jesus assures us that God is proactive.

Our heavenly Father sent Jesus to provide for the redemption of his creation, and we're invited to be part of that. It starts with our personal redemption as we repent. We receive his cleansing and new life, and then we listen for guidance so we'll be in step with his Spirit as we seek to do his will and make a difference. Right now it is happening all over the world as believers show mercy and love for the broken and the oppressed, communicating the good news that God so loved world he sent his Son.

The gateway to redemptive engagement is prayer.

The Only Way to Work

SELECTIONS FROM JOHN 5

> *But Jesus replied,*
> *"My Father is always working,*
> *and so am I."*

Father in heaven, it's fascinating to think about your being active all the time. What are you creating now? How are you working in us who are so in need of your grace? Are you disrupting the evil forces that plague us? How can we be part of your work?

Thank you for always being "up to something." Thank you for not simply watching us suffer. Thank you for blessing us with your Son and your Holy Spirit.

Help me, Lord, to be part of your work—to be active in accomplishing your will on earth as it is in heaven.

Guide me, cleanse me, equip me . . .

> *So Jesus explained,*
> *"I tell you the truth,*
> *The Son can do nothing by himself.*
> *He does only what he sees the Father doing."*

Lord, help me to see what you are doing, where you are active! Guide me to be present there and aware of how I can actively participate in what you're doing.

Help me to see how the good news of your grace is more powerful than all the world's hatred and evil. Allow me to be a messenger of your grace to others as I refuse to participate in hatred and evil.

Open my eyes to see wonderful things from your Word and to hear the whispers of your Holy Spirit. Enable me to work as Jesus works: doing only what I see the Father doing.

❦

A PRAYER FOR TODAY

Lead us not into temptation, but deliver us from evil. Whatever you have for me to do today, guide me, empower me, and keep me walking in step with your Spirit.

The Best Invitation

There was a certain time when I was particularly anxious about work and family pressures. Headlines about disasters and global threats kept eating at me. But then one morning I awoke slowly with these words resonating in me: *Love the Lord your God with all your heart, and with all your soul, and with all your mind, and with all your strength.*

I knew Jesus said this was the greatest commandment, but as I lay there, it didn't feel like a command. It was a wonderful *invitation*! It drew me into peace, and even buoyancy. Love *for* God and *from* God was filling my heart, soul, and mind.

A little later, as I was still savoring God's presence, the "invitation" blended with Isaiah's promise that "when our minds are stayed on the Lord, we're kept in perfect peace."

None of us can dodge life's pressures and fears. Yet our heavenly Father commands us to love him, for he loves us. And as we see in Psalm 119, God's commands are sources of empowerment and refreshment. Don't we all wish for more strength to face the day, and more times of rest? God provides exactly that.

Isaiah 26:3 promises, "You will keep in perfect peace all who trust in you, all whose thoughts are fixed on you!"

We may not all wake up sensing the commandment to love God is a blessed invitation. Yet as we "fix our thoughts on him," we can find that peace Isaiah describes.

—————— Bearing Fruit Everywhere ——————

SELECTIONS FROM COLOSSIANS 1

We always pray for you,
and we give thanks to God,
the Father of our Lord Jesus Christ.
For we have heard of your faith in Christ Jesus,
and your love for all of God's people. . . .

This same Good News that came to you
is going out all over the world.
It is bearing fruit everywhere by changing lives.

Father in heaven, as the endless troubles and violence in the world appear on our screens, thank you for the message that your good news is going out and bearing fruit by changing lives. Help us to see how your kingdom is all about that. Thank you that you're fulfilling your purposes through your good news and your love for "mere mortals."

So we have not stopped praying for you . . .
We ask God to give you complete knowledge
of his will
and to give you spiritual wisdom and
understanding.

You know the persons I'm praying for, Lord—hurting friends, friends of friends, family members, whole people groups. Pour out your grace on them. Work in their minds and hearts so that they, too, will see how your kingdom is coming. Lift their spirits. Reveal to them that this broken, tragic world is the scene of your good news.

Let them experience your love come alive in them—alive and well in all who call on your name.

We also pray that you will be strengthened
with all his glorious power
so you will have all the endurance and patience
*   you need.*
May you be filled with joy, always thanking the
*   Father.*

O, Lord, I need lots of endurance and patience! And joy? I experience too little of it! Your Word tells us joy comes from obedience and a spirit of gratitude and praise. Yes, I'm grateful, Father. I praise and thank you.

Please grant your grace and resilience to all the people I'm praying for. May they praise you and taste your joy.

⌁

A PRAYER FOR TODAY

Help me to love you, Lord, with all
my heart, and all my soul, and all
my mind, and all my strength.

The Music of Life

C. S. Lewis described George MacDonald as "constantly close to the Spirit of Christ," and Oswald Chambers wrote about MacDonald in a letter, "I love that writer." A prolific author and preacher, MacDonald had a sense of wonder about the love dynamic of Jesus and his Father; he wrote, "The Father loving the Son as only the Father can love, the Son loving the Father as only the Son can love. The prayer of the Lord for unity between men and the Father and himself springs from the eternal need of love. The more I regard it, the more I am lost in the wonder and glory of the thing."

MacDonald then makes it personal: "The very music that makes the harmony of life lies . . . in the burning love in the hearts of Father and Son . . . drawing us up into the glory of their joy."

In prayer we're brought into the dynamic love among Father, Son, and Spirit that transforms all that exists. In prayer we become part of the "family conversation," loving interactions made possible because Jesus came to bring amazing grace to our rebellious self-centeredness.

No wonder John, the beloved disciple, wrote so much about love in his letters . . .

The First Message

SELECTIONS FROM 1 JOHN 3

See how very much our Father loves us,
for he calls us his children,
and that is what we are! . . .

This is the message you have heard from the beginning:
We should love one another.

Father in heaven, I want to love you and others, including people different from me and those who annoy me. Pour your love into me, Lord, your love that is beyond my human love.

Dear children, let's not merely say we love each
other;
let us show the truth by our actions. . . .

And this is his commandment:
We must believe in the name of his Son,
Jesus Christ,
and love one another, just as he commanded us.
Those who obey God's commandments
remain in fellowship with him, and he with them.
And we know he lives in us
Because the Spirit he gave us lives in us.

Help me to be practical in showing love—and sometimes tough love—in this demanding world. Guide me to understand your commandments and to obey them.

Help me not to give mere lip service to love. When my beliefs are attacked, help me to love. When individuals stir up my anger, help me to love. When life seems unfair, help me to love. When I'm tired and hurting, still, help me to love.

Let nothing disturb my fellowship with you. Fill me with your Spirit and show me how to share your love with others.

❧

A PRAYER FOR TODAY

May my love be dynamic because it comes
from you, Creator and Redeemer.

DAY 17

Our True Nature

In *Journey of Prayer*, author Rosemary Budd echoes George MacDonald's sense of wonder about the love among the triune God: "God is love," she wrote. "The Father is always offering love to the Son, and this gift of love is the Son's glory, which he in turn perpetually offers to the Father. God lives in a relationship of love."

We all desire a relationship of love. Those raised in dysfunctional families often feel intense longing to be part of a family full of love and caring for each other. Spiritually, we have that kind of longing in our dysfunctions until we are brought into the circle of love with our heavenly Father.

MacDonald conveyed the idea that when we truly say with Jesus, "Thy will be done," then the life of the Father and the Son flow through us and we become true children of God. He emphasized that we are not made for self but for love. "Our neighbor is our refuge; self is our demon-foe. Every man is the image of God to every man, and in proportion as we love him, we shall know [that] sacred fact."

We need to hear MacDonald's message in our narcissistic culture!

The promise of Christ in us makes possible the audacious idea that we can pray as Jesus prayed, a genuine child of our heavenly Father, "Thy will be done."

Why We Love Each Other

SELECTIONS FROM 1 JOHN 4

*Dear Friends, let us continue to love one
    another,
for love comes from God.
Anyone who loves is a child of God and
    knows God.
But anyone who does not love
does not know God, for God is love.*

Father in heaven, since you are the source of authentic love, I open myself to you. Let me love you and others as you love your Son and all of us who call on your holy name. Help me to know you and to respond to your Spirit's guidance in sharing your love.

*God showed how much he loved us
by sending his one and only Son into the world
so that we might have eternal life through him.
This is real love—
not that we loved God,
but that he loved us . . .*

*Dear friends, since God loved us that much,
we surely ought to love each other. . . .*

We love each other because he loved us first.

Thank you, Father, for sending your Son so that we can have eternal life through him. Let your real love flow through me and to those I live with, work with, and worship with.

∽

A Prayer for Today

Lord, enable me to sense the reality of
your love for humanity. Help me to share
your love in fresh, unexpected ways.

DAY 18

Satan's Strategy

Helmut Thielicke, in his powerful book on the Lord's Prayer titled *Our Heavenly Father*, emphasizes that good things and even great things can get between the child and the Father. He identifies in Luther's hymn, "A Mighty Fortress Is Our God," the competitors to God's kingdom, and they're not the usual suspects of envy or hatred or sexual vice. No, Luther named "goods, fame, child, and wife." The nearness of God can be lost by elevating anything else above him, even good and virtuous things.

Thielicke was a pastor who faithfully served his congregation under persecution from the Nazis, so he had a unique understanding of Satan's wiles. "Dangers lurk in unexpected places, and . . . the wildest wolves that lie in wait for us wear the most harmless-looking sheep's clothing." He points out the tempter in the wilderness "made nothing but grand and captivating proposals to Jesus. He did not forget to appeal to his idealism, to his piety, and even the Word of God. . . . There was only one thing he wanted, and that was to separate him from the Father."

Thielicke puts his finger on the key issue—that Satan wanted to separate Jesus—and now us—from the Father.

How did Jesus resist the devil's temptations? He knew his identity—that he was the Father's Son—and he quoted the Scriptures. When temptations come at us, our identity as children of our heavenly Father gives us confidence. Saturating our minds and hearts with the Scriptures brings them to mind when tempted, instructing us on how we should respond as God's children.

Jesus "practiced the presence" of his Father. Practicing God's presence is the surest protection when we're tempted.

Confronting Temptation

SELECTIONS FROM MATTHEW 4

*Then Jesus was led by the Spirit into the wilderness
to be tempted there by the devil. . . .*

*"If you are the Son of God,
tell these stones to become loaves of bread."*

*But Jesus told him,
"No! The Scriptures say,*

*'People do not live by bread alone,
but by every word that comes from the mouth
of God.'"*

Lord, I don't know what temptations will come my way today, but please bring to my mind words from your Scriptures that pull me back onto your paths. When tempted, keep me from ignoring your commands and invitations, keep me from quenching your Spirit.

*Then the devil took him to the holy city, Jerusalem,
to the highest point of the Temple, and said,
"If you are the Son of God, jump off!
For the Scriptures say,*

'He will order his angels to protect you . . .'"

Jesus responded, "The Scriptures also say,
'You must not test the LORD your God . . .'"

"Get out of here, Satan. . . . For the Scriptures say,

'You must worship the LORD your God and serve
only him.'"

Our Father in heaven, help me pray like Jesus and let me worship and serve you and you only—not my own schemes and self-centered desires.

Protect me from the wiles of the Evil One, and let your words "dwell in me richly."

༄

A PRAYER FOR TODAY

As I deal with temptations today, please
bring words of Scripture to mind so
I can cope with whatever comes.

What Is Peace?

Someone has said, "Peace is not the absence of trouble but the presence of God."

That resonates with John 16 where Jesus says on earth his followers will have many "trials and sorrows," but they should "take heart." He knew that coming events would challenge their faith.

He told them the Father loves them dearly. He told them that their grief would be temporary. He told them they could experience peace in him.

How? Jesus emphasized we should ask the Father in his name so we could have "abundant joy."

As we see the wretchedness of refugees and victims of violence, many of us feel both empathy and anxiety. We endure personal loss and grief. It can all act as a kind of blackmail against the joy Jesus described.

When Jesus looked out at the crowds, he had compassion on them because they were confused and helpless—like so many in our culture. Yet he didn't let that drain his relationship with his Father. In that context he said, "The harvest is great, but the workers are few. So pray to the Lord who is in charge of the harvest; ask him to send more workers into his fields.".

So we are to become part of the Father's work. The world is full of trouble, but God is in charge of the harvest. Our prayers matter as we engage in bringing the good news of hope and redemption.

We can't escape trouble, even in our most protected and loving communities—it's part of the human condition. But we can experience God's peace.

Fear and Courage

SELECTIONS FROM MATTHEW 10

"Look, I am sending you out as sheep among wolves.
So be as shrewd as snakes and harmless as doves."

Sometimes, Lord, it's hard to take comfort in your words. Too many people these days are sheep among wolves and they get eaten alive! Soon it could be me and those I love.

Help me to see wolves the way you see them. Enable me to see all things through your eyes. Give me the awe at your glory that brings cleansing and wonder. Instruct me, Holy Spirit, so I can understand the realistic, hard things.

Grant me your shrewdness, not mine! Transform my fears into courage from you.

"What is the price of two sparrows—one copper coin?
But not a single sparrow can fall to the ground
without your Father knowing it.
And the very hairs on your head are all numbered.
So don't be afraid; you are more valuable to God
than a whole flock of sparrows."

How remarkable, Father, that you know everything about my body and my life . . . yet even more remarkable, that I am *valuable* to you. Help me to realize what this means and what I should do about it.

Give me, Lord, your boldness and wisdom.

Help me to pray in your Spirit for all who suffer and are lost in this troubled world.

⁄

A PRAYER FOR TODAY

Father, in Jesus' name I ask you to
breathe into me the presence of your
Spirit as I live today among wolves,
sheep, and searching souls.

"Don't Be Afraid"

A remarkable story told in Acts 16 speaks to our fears. Paul and Silas were ministering in Jesus' name when a mob formed against them. They were stripped and severely beaten with wooden rods, then thrown into prison. In the inner dungeon, their feet clamped in stocks, they didn't know what would happen to them next. Yet instead of groaning in misery from their wounds, they began praying and singing hymns to God. And then, miracles happened.

When we are in fear-filled circumstances, our inclination is to complain and to look around to find others who can share in our misery. We put our news in social media to draw sympathy and commiseration. What's a better remedy?

In the Scriptures we find that prayer and praise are antidotes to fear. For instance David, referring to a time of great danger, wrote in a psalm: "I will praise the LORD at all times. I will constantly speak his praises. I will boast only in the LORD; let all who are helpless take heart." Again and again we see in the Psalms utterances of praise despite grief and desperate circumstances.

On the other hand, a different kind of fear—fear of the Lord—leads to repentance and the courage to praise despite what's making us afraid.

Fear and Little Faith

SELECTIONS FROM LUKE 12

"Dear friends,
don't be afraid of those who want to kill your body;
they cannot do any more to you after that.
But I'll tell you whom to fear.
Fear God."

Almighty Lord of Creation, almost every day we see terrible images of the killings of men, women, and children—all of them made in your image. We feel this strange mixture of disbelief, numbness, and fear. Might it happen here? Will it happen to us? To me?

You've told us not to fear those who kill the body, but we see evidence of violence all over the world. Many are so vulnerable. We are vulnerable! We could experience horrific devastation. We could lose everything. We could become refugees.

So many bad things keep happening in our communities! What might shatter everything we hold dear? What will happen to me and to my loved ones?

"Can all your worries add a single moment to
your life? . . .

"Look at the lilies and how they grow . . .
Why do you have so little faith? . . .

"Seek the Kingdom of God above all else,
and he will give you everything you need.

"So don't be afraid, little flock.
For it gives your Father great happiness
to give you the Kingdom."

Open my eyes, Lord, to what you are promising. Life is short, but eternity and your kingdom are forever. Even if life goes pretty smoothly and I die of old age, my time in my body here is just the blink of an eye, a mist. But living in your kingdom of eternal adventures and authentic pleasures will never end.

How fascinating that you tell us your Father—our Father—gets "great pleasure" in including us. What a reason to give you praise and to rejoice!

Thank you, Lord, for grace, hope, and purpose.

∽

A PRAYER FOR TODAY

Lord, move in my mind and heart
with the health, wisdom, and
purpose of your Holy Spirit.

Jesus' Straight Talk about Prayer

It's clear that Jesus was fed up with the fake prayers of his religious community. In Matthew's gospel we see his sharp critique, his model for how to pray, and the requirement that we must forgive others. He urges we be persistent in prayer and expectant that our heavenly Father will respond.

MATTHEW 6:5—15; 7:7—11

When you pray, don't be like the hypocrites who love to pray publicly on street corners and in the synagogues where everyone can see them. I tell you the truth, that is all the reward they will ever get. But when you pray, go away by yourself, shut the door behind you, and pray to your Father in private. Then your Father, who sees everything, will reward you.

When you pray, don't babble on and on as the Gentiles do. They think their prayers are answered merely by repeating their words again and again. Don't be like them, for your Father knows exactly what you need before you ask him! Pray like this:

Our Father in heaven,
    may your name be kept holy.

May your Kingdom come soon.
May your will be done on earth,
> as it is in heaven.
Give us today the food we need,
and forgive us our sins,
> as we have forgiven those who sin against us.
And don't let us yield to temptation,
> but rescue us from the evil one.

If you forgive those who sin against you, your heavenly Father will forgive you. But if you refuse to forgive others, your Father will not forgive your sins. . . .

Keep on asking, and you will receive what you ask for. Keep on seeking, and you will find. Keep on knocking, and the door will be opened to you. For everyone who asks, receives. Everyone who seeks, finds. And to everyone who knocks, the door will be opened.

You parents—if your children ask for a loaf of bread, do you give them a stone instead? Or if they ask for a fish, do you give them a snake? Of course not! So if you sinful people know how to give good gifts to your children, how much more will your heavenly Father give good gifts to those who ask him.

PART THREE

Our Troubled Times

Job 5:7 gives us this vivid word picture of our common plight: "People are born for trouble as readily as sparks fly up from a fire."

Every day our screens dramatically demonstrate how true that is.

When we pray, "Your will be done on earth, as it is in heaven," we ask for what is hard to imagine actually happening. If the Father's will were being done on earth—if heavenly spirits were fully in charge, without a single evil spirit tempting and tormenting—what would life be like? If all the billions of humans were full of praise and love for the Creator and focused on doing his will, how mind-boggling would that be? How different would that look?

"Your will be done on earth . . ." When we pray those words, we ask that earth would be liberated from the powers of sin and evil. How? In Psalm 103 we get a glimpse of celestial beings carrying out the Father's will, "listening for each of his commands."

We, too, can listen for each command, for Jesus said the Holy Spirit would be our guide.

We can pray like the psalmist in Psalm 143: "Teach me to do your will, for you are my God. May your gracious spirit lead me forward." Note the word "gracious." The commands of God are not to constrict and make miserable but, as we see in the Psalms, they're like gold and bring joy.

Romans 12:2 tells us that God's will is "good and pleasing and perfect." Jesus was on a mission to bring God's will to earth. "For I have come down from heaven to do the will of God who sent me," Jesus said. From the time he was twelve and told his parents he had to "be about my Father's business" (as the King James Version puts it) and continuing throughout his ministry, he emphasized his Father's will. In his agony at Gethsemane he prayed, "Yet I want your will to be done, not mine."

Why the agony? Why the need for his mission from heaven to earth?

He taught us to pray, "rescue us from the evil one." Jesus was intensely aware of how much his Father's heaven contrasted with what the Evil One was doing on earth. We start these next ten days meditating on prayers for deliverance from the devil's wiles. May you find strength here for the daily battle and a refuge for the storms of life.

The Evil Commander

Jesus spoke from visceral experience when he taught us to pray, "Your will be done on earth, as it is in heaven." He knew the stark contrasts between his Father's kingdom and our fallen world. He endured Satan's wiles and temptations, and he cast demons out of the possessed. He knew the full extent of our human experience.

The Bible calls Satan "the god of this world" and says that the devil is "the commander of the powers in the unseen world." When Satan offered Jesus power and prestige on this planet, Jesus did not contradict him by saying, "This is my Father's world! What are you talking about?" He was fully aware of the devil's dominance in human affairs and that his evil minions were ceaselessly subverting the will of the Father.

In one way, it's hard to imagine that our beautiful earth is under so much influence from dark powers. At the same time, when we consider all the evil and hatred that we encounter on a daily basis, and when we see the extent of corrupted innocence, it's not at all hard to realize evil powers are manipulating from "the unseen world."

The Daily Battle

SELECTIONS FROM EPHESIANS 6

Be strong in the Lord and in his mighty power.
Put on all of God's armor
so that you will be able to stand firm
against all strategies of the devil.
For we are not fighting against flesh-and-blood
enemies,
but against evil rulers and authorities of the
unseen world,
against mighty powers in this dark world,
and against evil spirits in the heavenly places.

Lord, your Word tells me your armor is your truth, righteousness, and peace. All of that must come from you, for I'm painfully aware my righteousness is as filthy rags. Fill me, I pray, with love for your truth. Cleanse me, and clothe me with your righteousness. Bring into my mind and heart the peace that comes with your presence.

Hold up the shield of faith
to stop the fiery arrows of the devil.
Put on salvation as your helmet,
and take the sword of the Spirit,
which is the word of God.

Father in heaven, thank you for your Word's instructions and power. Put within me the faith that I'll need to stop those fiery arrows. Yes, they keep coming at me! Fill my being with the strength and power and love of your Holy Spirit so evil forces stop subverting your will in my life.

*Pray in the Spirit
at all times and on every occasion.
Stay alert and be persistent
in your prayers for all believers everywhere.*

Lord, not only for my sake but for those I'm praying for, guide my thoughts and my prayers so that they are pleasing in your sight.

～

A Prayer for Today

Equip me, Lord, with your full armor
so I will not be a casualty of evil forces
but an instrument of your peace.

"All Shall Be Well"

As he fought Apartheid in his native South Africa, Alan Paton, author of the classic novel *Cry, the Beloved Country*, at times felt despair at the uncompromising injustice he saw. Talk about troubled times! Yet he wrote that when he prayed the prayer of St. Francis, "my melancholy is dispelled, my self-pity comes to an end, my faith is restored, because of the majestic conception of what the work of a disciple should be."

"The work of a disciple!" Jesus charged his disciples to engage in his Father's work, and Paton and St. Francis found it life-changing—and life-giving.

For Paton, praying to become God's instrument of peace meant "Life is no longer nasty, mean, brutish, and short, but becomes the time that one needs to make it less nasty and mean." He kept working for justice and peace, saying to himself, "this is the only way in which a Christian can encounter hatred, injury, despair, and sadness, and that is by throwing off his helplessness and allowing himself to be made the bearer of love, the pardoner, the bringer of hope, the comforter of those that grieve."

When tempted to despair at hatred and injustice, we too might be inspired by the power of the deceptively simple prayer of St. Francis:

Lord, make me an instrument of your peace.
Where there is hatred, let me sow love; where there
is injury, pardon; where there is doubt, faith; where
there is despair, hope; where there is darkness, light;
where there is sadness, joy.

Amazing Justice

SELECTIONS FROM PSALM 96

Sing a new song to the LORD!
  Let the whole earth sing to the LORD!
Sing to the LORD; praise his name.
  Each day proclaim the good news that he saves.
Publish his glorious deeds among the nations.
  Tell everyone about the amazing things he does.
Great is the LORD! He is most worthy of praise!

It is so good to praise you, Lord! No matter what our troubles and
no matter what events on our screens or in our neighborhoods
bewilder us, we can still sing to you and praise your name.

You have given us the good news that you are redeeming us
and all your creation. For so many in our nation and in our world,
justice seems impossible, an outrageous mockery. Millions are
oppressed or imprisoned—yet you are at work in unseen ways.

Lord, do your amazing things. Rescue the oppressed, and let
each of us who follow you become instruments of your peace. In
tragic events, let your good news bring souls alive to your presence.

Worship the LORD in all his holy splendor.
Let all the earth tremble before him. . . .
He will judge all peoples fairly.

Let the heavens be glad, And the earth rejoice!

How amazing is your justice, Lord. So much on earth is unfair. But you judge everyone fairly. I rejoice that you are the God of justice, love, and redemption.

Help me to echo Julian of Norwich's assurance that "All shall be well, and all manner of things shall be well." I am glad. I rejoice.

Yet, Lord, I yearn for all this to be evident and I yearn to be part of your work. You know how I'm distressed by doubts and acutely aware of my weaknesses. You know how frail I am.

They say prayer is for the helpless. I need you every hour, Lord. Grant me the presence of your Holy Spirit, so I can rejoice and be glad indeed.

⌒

A Prayer for Today

Father in heaven, help me to sense
your presence hour by hour and to
rejoice in your goodness and grace.

When Someone Betrays You

Betrayal comes in many forms, and it is far from rare. When someone we trust betrays us, we can be shaken to the core.

In marriage we are nakedly vulnerable to the deep wounds of unexpected rejection and divorce. At work, where we spend so many hours of our lives, colleagues may spin events in cruel ways. Betrayals in church relationships, where we are encouraged to expose our truest selves, can devastate faith. Siblings, best friends, teammates . . . betrayal feels like a stunning dart to the gut.

When someone dear to us or someone we trusted betrays us, how should we pray?

When Jesus was betrayed by Judas, his constant prayer life with his Father enabled him to accept the harsh reality and move on with his mission. When Jesus knew Peter would deny him he told him, "Simon, Simon, Satan has asked to sift each of you like wheat. But I have pleaded in prayer for you, Simon, that your faith should not fail."

Jesus knew how determined the evil powers were to shake all his disciples, and he "pleaded in prayer" for them. Yet he accepted that God allowed Judas to be taken over by Satan.

Sometimes betrayal brings searing pain. Sometimes we hardly know how to pray about it. Jesus models praying against the Evil One, and praying for those Satan wants to "sift like wheat."

Pleading in Prayer

SELECTIONS FROM LUKE 22

Jesus said,
"I have been very eager
to eat this Passover meal with you
before my suffering begins. . . .

But here at this table,
sitting among us as a friend,
is the man who will betray me.
For it has been determined
that the Son of Man must die."

Lord, your focus on your mission and your determination to complete your Father's will speaks to me about what my focus should be. Help me to see the way you view those in my life who inflict pain. Guide me in the ways I should be thinking. Show me how to respond and pray when I feel wounded.

"Simon, Simon, Satan has asked
to sift each of you like wheat.
But I have pleaded in prayer for you, Simon,
that your faith should not fail."

Father in heaven, is Satan trying to sift all of us like wheat? Please protect me from the clever ways he tries to separate me from you. Help me to see others who distress me as the devil's targets who need to be prayed for. Put passion and compassion in me, Lord, so I care enough to plead in prayer for others.

A PRAYER FOR TODAY

Holy Spirit of God, flow into me your love
for others as I walk with you this day.

DAY 24

Is Joy Possible?

In his book *Great Joy* theologian J. I. Packer asserts that joy is a habit.

A habit? How can that be?

Packer first celebrates joy: "The Christian life, though no joy-ride, is itself a joy road, leading through great joy here to greater joy hereafter. . . . Joy is truly life-transforming." He advocates "a supreme concentration on the source of joy" to make a personal practice of joy possible, despite the daily bad news and troubles.

Then he gets practical and unpacks seven habits to build: *lifting* our eyes to God in wonder and gratitude; *leaving behind* self-absorption and self-pity; *looking ahead* toward our joyful future in heaven; *loving* the Lord's mercy, wisdom, faithfulness and grace; *singing* psalms and hymns; *enjoying* God's creation of flowers, trees, streams, and all things of natural beauty; *loving* your neighbor.

Building good joy habits, like any exercise, requires focus. We have to intentionally clear away other distractions, devote time and energy, and persist through the pain. Packer counsels that we supremely concentrate on God as we walk "the path to the personal practice of joy." Building that habit gives us a fresh way of thinking about and acting upon what Jesus meant when he said he had come that we might have joy.

From Mourning to Dancing

SELECTIONS FROM PSALM 30

Sing to the LORD, all you godly ones!
  Praise his holy name.
For his anger lasts only a moment,
  but his favor lasts a lifetime!
Weeping may last through the night,
  but joy comes in the morning.

Thank you for the realism of this psalm, Lord, with joy and mourning so mixed. You said you came to bring us joy, yet your life here was as a "man of sorrows, acquainted with deepest grief." Help me to live your way in this strange mix of weeping and joy. Fix my eyes above—even when I feel anxious and have plenty of reasons to weep.

When I was prosperous, I said,
  "Nothing can stop me now!" . . .
Then you turned away from me, and I was
  shattered.

Father in heaven, the psalmist's experience seems so familiar. There are times when much is going right and then, suddenly, my failure or some calamity shatters my momentum and my sense of your blessings.

  Thank you that failure and weeping is not the end of my story. Help me, Lord, to keep my eyes on you.

You have turned my mourning into joyful dancing.
  You have taken away my clothes of mourning
    and clothed me with joy.
That I might sing praises to you . . .
  O LORD my God, I will give you thanks forever!

93

Thank you, Lord, for this encouragement. All praise to you, Lord, for you come to us when we are mourning and you bring us your joy.

⌒

A Prayer for Today

Help me today to build the habit of praise
and joy. Let me rejoice in your beautiful
creation and in your redemption and love.

DAY 25

Look for the Fun

A woman with more than her share of troubles was determined to keep a twinkle in her eye. She had barely survived a series of cancer treatments, and her daughter, when entering adolescence, was diagnosed with schizophrenia. As the years went by, the woman's cancer kept reoccurring, her hospitalized daughter sustained serious injuries from a knife attack by a deranged patient, and her husband endured job losses. Yet as a great believer in the promises of Scripture, she kept saying with a smile, "Look for the fun!"

And she did. She lived with a mix of realism and hope, being faithful in prayer and trusting in her heavenly Father.

In a world of so much pain, confusion, and tragedy, the Scriptures tell us we are to embrace joy; it should *fill* us. In Scripture, the outpouring of joy includes celebration: feasting, playing instruments, singing, dancing, shouting, clapping, giving gifts.

And Jesus came to give us joy. Fun and humor may seem frivolous, yet scholars have long shown how Jesus used humor to make his points and how he ministered during celebrations. We may live in tough times and experience sobering things, but looking for the fun and, as the saying goes, seeing the glass half full, can be part of keeping in step with the Spirit.

Despite our discouragements, we can respond to Paul's advice in Philippians . . .

Retrain the Brain

SELECTIONS FROM PHILIPPIANS 4

*Always be full of joy in the Lord. I say it again—
rejoice!
Let everyone see that you are considerate in all
you do . . .*

*Don't worry about anything; instead, pray about
everything.
Tell God what you need, and thank him for all he
has done.
Then you will experience God's peace, which
exceeds anything we can understand.
His peace will guard your hearts and minds as you
live in Christ Jesus.*

Lord, I love this promise of peace beyond my understanding. Yet as I tell you all I need and thank you for all you have done, I know I often don't measure up. I don't always pray about everything, and I'm not always in tune with you.

Please help me right now to sense your presence. Bring your joy into my mind and soul. Show me the ways today to experience your joy and peace.

*And now, dear brothers and sisters, one final thing.
Fix your thoughts on what is true,
and honorable, and right, and pure, and lovely,
and admirable.*

Think about things that are excellent and worthy of praise.

Lord, you know all the thoughts flowing through my mind. It's full of stuff that doesn't match up to what's described in these verses. Help me to focus on what comes from you—on what's honorable and pure and worthy of praise.

All praise to you, Father, for loving us enough to promise your presence and answer our prayers.

⁓

A PRAYER FOR TODAY

All through this day, Lord, help me to be filled with joy. Let me fix my thoughts on excellent things that bring you pleasure.

Prayer in Disaster

In Jesus' time—in all times—wars and natural disasters have shattered communities and people's lives. Might it happen to us? And how would we react if it did? We hope that under the tremendous pressure of catastrophic circumstances we would have strength and courage and unswerving faith, that we wouldn't despair.

In Germany during the Thirty Years' War, Martin Rinkart lived through enemy invasion, starvation, disease, and widespread death. He gave us a remarkable example of living with faith and hope in horrific circumstances. As the only surviving pastor in his walled city, he conducted up to fifty funerals a day. Yet he kept writing hymns, among them, "Now Thank We All Our God."

His hymn includes these words:

Now thank we all our God, with heart and hands
    and voices,
Who wondrous things has done, in whom his world
    rejoices; . . .
Oh, may this bounteous God through all our life
    be near us,
With ever joyful hearts and blessed peace to cheer us;
And keep us in His grace, and guide us when
    perplexed;

And free us from all ills in this world and the next.
All praise and thanks to God the Father now be
    given . . .

Considering all the "ills in this world," we may be mightily
perplexed these days. Yet as we pray for grace and guidance, and
as we express praise and thanks to our heavenly Father, we may
experience some of what kept Martin Rinkart faithful.

Unshaken

SELECTIONS FROM PSALM 16

*Keep me safe, O God,
    for I have come to you for refuge.*

*I said to the LORD, "You are my Master!
    Every good thing I have comes from you."
The godly people in the land
    are my true heroes!
    I take pleasure in them!*

Lord, when I am anxious about what could happen, help me to
remember that you are my refuge. Good things come from you,
and from "godly people in the land."

Ours is a wonderful heritage! Father in heaven, thank you for
your wondrous gift of loving us as your children.

Yes, those who serve you are the true heroes! I take pleasure
right now in praying for them, that you will grant them peace and
resilience despite the things that rough up their lives.

*LORD, you alone are my inheritance, my cup of
    blessing.
You guard all that is mine.*

The land you have given me is a pleasant land.
What a wonderful inheritance!

I will bless the LORD who guides me;
even at night my heart instructs me.
I know the LORD is always with me.
I will not be shaken, for he is right beside me.

. . . You will show me the way of life,
granting me the joy of your presence
and the pleasures of living with you forever.

Father in heaven, please guide me as I try to process yesterday, persevere through today, and ponder tomorrow. I need so much guidance, so much wisdom in life's complexity. Grant me the joy of your presence. Help me to obey the whispers of your Holy Spirit.

May your presence in me keep me unshaken, whatever happens around me and to my loved ones.

∽

A PRAYER FOR TODAY

Grant me, Lord, resilience and courage
as I keep my eyes on you and invite you
into my thoughts throughout the day.

DAY 27

Shouting into Silence

On the cross, Jesus called out with a loud voice, "My God, my God, why have you abandoned me?" David's Psalm 22 starts with those very words: "My God, my God, why have you abandoned me?" and continues: "Why are you so far away when I groan for help? Every day I call to you, my God, but you do not answer. Every night I lift my voice, but I find no relief."

Jesus quoted the Psalms more than any other Old Testament book.

And the Psalms are the most-read book in the Bible. We read the Psalms because of their eyes-wide-open authenticity.

Theologians have always wrestled with "the silence of God." If he is almighty, why do our prayers often seem unanswered? Why in terrible times do we sometimes feel abandoned by our Father in heaven?

Jesus on the cross, after shouting into the silence, released his spirit. Three days later he rose from the grave, having fulfilled his Father's will—changing everything.

When we shout into the silence, when we pray in our grief or fear, we may feel abandoned. Yet we see in the Psalms—and in Jesus' life, death, and resurrection—the mysteries of our faith. In Psalm 22 David dramatically shifts from his sense of abandonment to prophecies about Jesus' passion and hope: "Praise the

Lord, all you who fear him! . . . For he has not ignored or belittled the suffering of the needy. He has not turned his back on them, but has listened to their cries for help."

Do not lose hope. God's apparent silence is neither apathy nor inaction.

Has God Forgotten me?

Selections from Psalm 77

I cry out to God; yes, I shout.
    Oh, that God would listen to me! . . .
I think of God, and I moan,
    overwhelmed with longing for his help. . . .

I think of the good old days . . .
    when my nights were filled with joyful songs. . . .
Has the Lord rejected me forever?
    Will he never again be kind to me? . . .
Has God forgotten to be gracious?
    Has he slammed the door on his compassion?

Father in heaven, how can so many things go so wrong these days? Are you really listening to us? How can we experience your joy when so much pain and anxiety darkens life for so many?

We long for your mighty hand to bring showers of grace and mercy in our storms of adversity. Lord, how long must we wait?

And I said, "This is my fate;
    the Most High has turned his hand against me."
But then I recall all you have done, O Lord;
    I remember your wonderful deeds of long ago

Yes, Lord, I do remember times when your grace and love flowed into my life. And I'm thinking now of your mighty works shown in the Scriptures and of Jesus' promises of being with us. Help me to focus on your love and your purposes.

Change my dismay and bewilderment into resilient faith. You know so well that I can't generate that myself! Do your wonderful works in me and through me. Fill me with your Holy Spirit.

Right now I bring before you all my loved ones and all those who are going through rough times. Bless and encourage them. Break apart the log jams that make their lives miserable. Bring them hope and courage and wisdom.

And, Lord, in the terrible tragedies of this world, bring your justice and your care and your spiritual renewal into the lives of every soul. We look for your redemption, Father, and your wonderful works in your suffering creation.

თ

A Prayer for Today

I remember all the wonderful things you've
done, and I'm looking for your surprises
today as I live in the hope of the gospel.

In Heaven's Light

Jesus made it clear that heaven is a real place when he told his followers he would prepare a place for them. Having come from heaven, he had a vivid sense of what it was like, yet we don't see in the Gospels that he spent time describing it.

Can you imagine a New Yorker describing Manhattan to remote islanders about to visit the big city? The New York native might sketch images of the Empire State Building, Central Park, and Times Square, yet what about the police, mass media, and political conflicts? What about the arts, the shopping, and the subway? What would be most important for the islanders to know?

Jesus emphasized that the most important thing about heaven was the fact his Father was there. Images of golden streets and trumpeting angels fade beside Jesus' emphasis that in heaven we will be welcomed home by our Father—and that starts right now. He advised we store our treasures in heaven, warned we must forgive others so our Father in heaven will forgive us, and said that those who do the will of his Father are the ones who will enter heaven.

Jesus lived with a two-world perspective, and he calls us to share his worldview. Yet the glories and welcome of heaven can seem distant in competition with our wired, colorful, demanding world. We may hear wonderful things about heaven, yet our dread of death may make us shove its realities to the backs of our minds.

Some have likened our brief stay on earth to schooling for heaven, and to death as graduation. We see graduating students exuberantly throw their caps into the air in celebration. The hard part is over, and they're ready to reap the promised benefits.

Do we view our entrance into heaven that way? Jesus knew earth was in stark contrast to his "native country" with his Father. What are our expectations of what's ahead after our brief sojourn here, and how does that affect our thoughts and actions now?

New Life Forever

SELECTIONS FROM 1 PETER 1

May God give you more and more grace and peace.

. . . Now we live with great expectation,
and we have a priceless inheritance—
an inheritance that is kept in heaven for you,
pure and undefiled, beyond the reach of change
and decay.

Lord, please give me "the mind of Christ" about this life and the life to come. Help me to live with "great expectation" about my future inheritance and to genuinely sense your grace and peace.

So be truly glad.
There is wonderful joy ahead,
even though you must endure many trials for a
little while.
These trials will show that your faith is genuine. . . .

For you have been born again,
but not to a life that will quickly end.
Your new life will last forever.

It's hard for me to imagine living forever, Lord. What will my life actually be like? How different will my body be? How many of those descriptions of heaven in books and movies match up to what I'll experience?

I love the images of coming to the warm home of my heavenly Father.

Help me, Lord, to focus on the essentials about heaven—about your grace and righteousness and redemption.

❧

A Prayer for Today

Father in heaven, keep me in step with
your Spirit today with that inner sense
that there is wonderful joy ahead.

DAY 29

Mortal, yet in God's Image

We read in the third chapter of Ecclesiastes, "God has made everything beautiful for its own time. He has planted eternity in the human heart."

God made us to live forever. We long for all those we love and all that we enjoy to continue on and on—yet our lives are brief. Even when someone dies in old age, we feel loss and unease about death's strangeness.

"Life is a short and fevered rehearsal for a concert we cannot stay to give," A. W. Tozer wrote. "Just when we have appeared to have attained some proficiency we are forced to lay our instruments down. There is simply not time enough to think, to become, to perform what the constitution of our natures indicates we are capable of."

Tozer added, "How completely satisfying to turn from our limitations to a God who has none."

We were created for eternity. We're the paradox of being mortal, yet made in God's image to be forever alive.

Jesus in his mortal body was acutely aware of life's brevity, and he focused on using his short time on earth to fulfill what his Father had sent him to do. That's why he was in constant contact with his Father.

The last chapter of Ecclesiastes emphasizes exactly that sort of focus during our own brief lifetime.

Do It Now

SELECTIONS FROM ECCLESIASTES 12

Don't let the excitement of youth
cause you to forget your Creator.
Honor him in your youth before you grow old
    and say,
"Life is not pleasant anymore." . . .

Remember him
before the door to life's opportunities is
    closed. . . .

Remember him before you near the grave.

How easy it is, Lord, to rush through my day and forget about you—to live by my common sense and my own will. Break into my thoughts and lift my eyes to the wonders of your creation and your love for us. Help me to remember that you invite me to knock at your door and that you will answer.

Fear God and obey his commands,
for this is everyone's duty.
God will judge us for everything we do.

Help me, heavenly Father, to both love you and fear you—to take you seriously. Give me the power to do what I know you want me to do and to listen for what you have to say to me.

Thank you, Lord, for your Scriptures that show me the way and the path you have for me.

~

A Prayer for Today

When today I have breaks and pauses,
help me to practice your presence and
to remember you are with me.

Fly to Safety?

Today we hear stories of people seriously prepping for cataclysmic events. They stockpile food and weapons and ready their SUVs to drive deep into mountain hideaways.

David in Psalm 11 is brutally frank about evil, violence, and the collapse of order. He addresses with bold faith the anxieties and despair of troubled times and affirms that, despite wickedness and injustice, the Lord still rules from heaven. Despite the dangers from his enemies, David rejects advice to flee to somewhere safe.

The plans of today's stockpilers match the advice of David's friends who advised him to "fly like a bird to the mountains for safety!" But David's first words in this psalm are, "I trust the LORD for protection."

Truth is, there is no safety in the mountains. Sometimes it's wise to flee violence and engage our survival instincts, but ultimately, our times and our lives are in the hands of the Lord.

When we fear the chilling scenarios depicted in movies, books, and the day's news, we can let those fears become catalysts for prayer . . . and catalysts for faith that looking to the Lord for protection is a better strategy than loading up those SUVs.

Someone's Watching

SELECTIONS FROM PSALM 11

I trust in the LORD for protection.
So why do you say to me,
  "Fly like a bird to the mountains for safety! . . .
The foundations of law and order have collapsed.
  What can the righteous do?"

Lord, we constantly see and hear how much the words of this psalm reflect what's going on. The question of what we should do is always hanging in the air. Guide us, we pray, and give us the courage and wisdom we need in this hour.

But the LORD is in his holy Temple;
  the LORD still rules from heaven.
He watches everyone closely,
  examining every person on earth.
The LORD examines both the righteous and the wicked. . . .
For the righteous LORD loves justice.
  The virtuous will see his face.

Yes, Lord, give us the faith to believe that you still rule and that your eyes are on the righteous. Bring your justice to earth, and may your will be done.

ℭℴ

A PRAYER FOR TODAY

When we hear of wickedness against innocent
people—when we are made aware of trafficking
and modern slavery and brutalities—help us to
somehow be instruments of your peace.

Jesus Praying

Sprinkled throughout the Gospels are mentions of Jesus prioritizing prayer despite the demands of ministering to large crowds and meeting their needs for spiritual and physical healing. The following passage from Matthew includes Jesus' prayers in the garden of Gethsemane.

MATTHEW 26:36–45 ESV

Then Jesus went with them to a place called Gethsemane, and he said to his disciples, "Sit here, while I go over there and pray." And taking with him Peter and the two sons of Zebedee, he began to be sorrowful and troubled. Then he said to them, "My soul is very sorrowful, even to death; remain here, and watch with me." And going a little farther he fell on his face and prayed, saying, "My Father, if it be possible, let this cup pass from me; nevertheless, not as I will, but as you will." And he came to the disciples and found them sleeping. And he said to Peter, "So, could you not watch with me one hour? Watch and pray that you may not enter into temptation. The spirit indeed is willing, but the flesh is weak." Again, for the second time, he went away and prayed, "My Father, if this cannot pass unless I drink it, your will be done." And again he came and found them sleeping, for their eyes were heavy. So, leaving them again, he went away and prayed for the third time, saying the same words again. Then he came to the disciples and said to them, "Sleep and take your rest later on. See, the hour is at hand, and the Son of Man is betrayed into the hands of sinners."

~∽

PART FOUR

Jesus in Trouble

Jesus' mission on earth thrust him into horrific battles with the evil powers. In his time of greatest crisis, with his crucifixion just hours away, he told his disciples he was "deeply troubled."

The remarkable fact is, we know many specifics of how he prayed in the ultimate showdown with the Evil One. John—the disciple Jesus especially loved—lets us listen in on the prayers of Jesus in the garden of Gethsemane when he faced betrayal, a mockery of a trial, and death.

When we feel overwhelmed by troubles and tempted to despair, we can see how the Son of God prayed in the midst of his greatest crisis. The range of his concerns is instructive, extending well beyond his own dread. We are privileged to meditate on how his extraordinary prayers relate to our prayers and to our lives now.

For the next several days we'll consider those prayers found in John 17. We will hear the intimate heart cries of the Savior when he was hours away from the cross. We will be moved by his primary concerns, his passionate love for his followers, and his candor with his Father. His prayers open unique windows through which we can glimpse the ultimate mysteries. On a practical level, we will see his concerns and join him in his prayers.

What's My Role?

Most of us have heard a coach or preacher say, "Make your life count for something." Jesus at Gethsemane, knowing he would soon be with his Father again, said to him, "I have completed all you sent me to do."

Talk about a life counting for something! How did Jesus figure out all he was to do during his time on earth? How did he keep his focus?

He kept talking to his Father. Jesus said he could do nothing by himself. He needed to know what the Father was doing so he could participate in it.

In our troubled times, in light of overwhelming needs and our limited time, energy, and resources, how do we focus? If we keep our focus on the world's needs, conflicting voices and demands make us wonder how to live with authentic faith. How can we make our lives count for something as our heavenly Father views it?

Like Jesus, we need to keep communicating with our heavenly Father. We need to stay prayerfully focused on what God gives us to do, even when it's difficult.

Jesus was intent on bringing glory to his Father. He had done all he had come to do, except the last, hardest thing. His prayers near the completion of his mission to redeem the world provide us with applicable insights: completing God's work on earth brings glory to the Father; Jesus reveals the Father to believers; and everything we have is a gift from our heavenly Father.

Bringing Glory on Earth

SELECTIONS FROM JOHN 17

*"I brought glory to you here on earth
by completing the work you gave me to do.
Now, Father, bring me into the glory
we shared before the world began."*

Father in heaven, here is my work. It's hard for me to see how it's significant. Show me how you view it and how I should do it, or change . . .

Here are my relationships and all my activities. Help me to practice your presence all through this day so that my work becomes genuinely meaningful.

*"I have revealed you to the ones
you gave me from this world.
They were always yours. . . .
Now they know that everything I have
is a gift from you . . .
They . . . know that I came from you,
and they believe you sent me."*

Yes, Lord, you have given me so many gifts, starting with life itself! Thank you for your invitation to fellowship with you. Knowing I'm yours and part of your loving family is the gift that transcends all others.

Thank you, Father, for sending your Son and for revealing him to us. Help us to be fully engaged in your work in the world just as he was.

⌒

A Prayer for Today

Father in heaven, help me today to sense
your presence and your love hour by
hour as I do all that is before me.

DAY 32

Prayer for Fellow Believers

If we are to pray like Jesus, we will be praying for others. Philip Yancey once wrote that if he had to answer the question "Why pray?" in one sentence, it would be, "Because Jesus did." We can apply that to intercessory prayer. We pray for our brothers and sisters in Christ as we see that Jesus prayed for his followers and for all who loved him.

When we worship with others, and when we get to know them and their stories, we become acutely aware of spiritual battles and the impact of our rough world on their lives and souls. We are all in need of prayer.

When we read of what's happening to believers all over the world, we see countless opportunities to pray for them. We may see few observable results in those we pray for near or far, and we may wonder if our prayers make any difference. Yet Jesus modeled intercessory prayer, and he emphasized we should ask with persistence and faith, believing our prayers will be answered according to our Father's will.

United Dynamism

SELECTIONS FROM JOHN 17

"All who are mine belong to you,
and you have given them to me,
so they bring me glory."

Thank you, Lord, for your grace in the lives of my brothers and sisters in Christ. Bless them today and give them a sense of your presence. Thank you for your promise that we belong to you.

Sometimes our spiritual battles are fierce. In temptations and confusions, please bring us your comfort and resilience and faith. Help us all, collectively and individually, to bring glory to you.

"Now I am departing from the world;
they are staying in this world . . .
protect them by the power of your name
so that they will be united just as we are."

Yes, Lord, please protect us and unite us in love for you and for each other. Help us to pray for other believers who consider our theology and our worldview wrongheaded.

Help us to love them as you love them. May our witness to the world be one of love and mercy, and not of judgment and condemnation so that your name is praised.

Father in heaven, here we are, "staying in this world," and we need your protection! Shield us from all the temptations and fiery darts of the Evil One. Protect us from what entices us away from you. Help us to be united in faith and your love.

❧

A PRAYER FOR TODAY

Dearest Jesus, protect me today by the power of
your name, and give me a passion for unity.

DAY 33

Joy and Hatred

Jesus told his followers he had come that they might have joy.
Clearly, that didn't mean he was promising Disney happiness
in a transformed culture. He came into a world of hatred and
violence. From soon after his birth, when Herod tried to kill him,
to his ministry years, when religious leaders plotted against him,
he experienced the world's enmity.

Yet throughout his life he brought joy. Mary with her cousin
Elizabeth, awestruck shepherds, wise men from the east, and during his ministry years the sick and the possessed healed by his
touch—all these and many others were struck with wonder and joy.

And still, as in our day, the forces of evil were always at work.

In Jesus' prayer, he says to his Father that he does not "belong
to the world" and that his followers will be hated because they are
not of this world either. Why? The world's ways are incompatible
with God's purity, goodness, and holiness. The world rejects us
when we follow Jesus.

Though the world may hate us, we are called not to retaliate,
but to love.

We are to model Jesus. Knowing he would soon be with his
Father, yet first having to endure the cross, he was not filled with

hatred for his betrayer or for his tormentors. On the cross he prayed that his Father would forgive them.

Joy comes from being in tune with our heavenly Father, whatever our circumstances.

Safe from Evil

SELECTIONS FROM JOHN 17

"Now I am coming to you.
I told them many things
while I was with them in this world
So they would be filled with my joy."

Lord Jesus, you have told us many things as recorded by your followers. Thank you for all your teachings, for your suffering for us, and for your redemption. Thank you that our reconciliation with you brings joy.

"I have given them your word.
And the world hates them
because they do not belong to the world,
just as I do not belong to the world.
I'm not asking you to take them out of the world,
but to keep them safe from the evil one."

Father, we see in our world so much wreckage from the Evil One! In your mercy, lift us from the wreckage.

Lift me from the wreckage I have caused!

Lift us from the wreckage all around us.

Cleanse me, Lord. Teach me, and fill me with your Spirit, so that I might be an instrument of your peace in a troubled land . . .

let not your heart be troubled

A PRAYER FOR TODAY

In the midst of the world's hatred, may I
respond with your love, forgiveness, and joy.

Holiness: Wholeness

Our culture has infected the word *holiness* with hostile meanings. It's been caricatured as cranky, narrow-minded, and bigoted, making most people wary of it. From superficial entertainment to serious novels, holiness has been depicted as religious extremism.

Yet holiness is wholeness and spiritual health! It flows from harmony with our Creator. Jesus prayed that those who belong to him would be "made holy."

How are we to be made holy?

We see in Jesus' prayer that it starts by seeking truth from the Father through his Word. It deepens by communicating with the Father so that we keep learning and applying his truth. Through this enormous privilege of open access to our Father through prayer, we are drawn into the blessed fellowship of the Trinity.

Imagine being warmed and inspired by sitting near a blazing fire. Far, far more will we be warmed and inspired and cleansed—made holy—by communing with our heavenly Father and his Spirit.

Jesus' prayer that we be "made holy" calls us to spiritual vitality. Nothing will make us feel more alive and energized than holiness.

Sent into the World

SELECTIONS FROM JOHN 17

*"They do not belong to this world any more than
 I do.
Make them holy by your truth;
teach them your word, which is truth."*

Lord, please open your Word to me, and help me to apply it as
you teach me what it really means. Let your Word and your truth
permeate my thoughts and my soul. Let your Word move my heart
and give me strength to do your will.

*"Just as you sent me into the world,
 I am sending them into the world.
And I give myself as a holy sacrifice for them
so they can be made holy by your truth."*

You know how troubled I am, Lord, by what's happening in this
world. It's hard to see how my prayers and my life can make much
of a difference. Please help me to fulfill your will and to grow more
and more into understanding and applying your truth.

May your holiness and health and spiritual wholeness flow
into and through me!

༕

A PRAYER FOR TODAY

Lord, let the precious promises and guidance
from your Word dominate my thoughts
today, leading me to greater holiness.

What Awes Us?

"That's awesome." The phrase has been used so often it now brings to mind the ordinary appreciation of a good cup of coffee instead of the vastness of unreachable galaxies or the trillions of unique snowflakes or the fascinating intricacies of the human body. It's easy to become jaded about galaxies and snowflakes when we see so many clips and photos of extraordinary phenomena.

It's equally easy to become jaded about what should make us feel even greater awe.

In today's meditation Jesus says to his Father that he is not only praying for his disciples but for all who believe in him.

That's us.

Jesus' praying for us is extraordinary.

When people we barely know say they're praying for us, we give it little thought. When persons of deep faith who take prayer seriously tell us they'll be praying for us, we take heart. How much more, then, do we take heart when we see this in the Scriptures: Jesus is interceding for us.

That's authentically awesome.

Our part is to listen to the quiet voice of the Holy Spirit and to respond with obedience and faith . . . and to pray that his love for us will fuel our love for him.

—————————— They in Us ——————————

SELECTIONS FROM JOHN 17

"I am praying not only for these disciples
but also for all who will ever believe in me."

You know, Lord, how much I need your prayers. The fact that you pray for me and for all who believe in you goes way beyond my understanding!

I heartily thank you for your love and your care for me. Help me today to respond to your prayers with love for you and others.

"I pray that they will all be one,
just as you and I are one—
as you are in me, Father, and I am in you.
And may they be in us
so that the world will believe you sent me."

Lord Jesus Christ, Son of God, the love you have for your Father and your oneness with him is far beyond my comprehension, but it challenges me to think of your honoring each other and the creative, empowering dynamic of your relationship.

Help me, Lord, to be one with you! Help me to be so immersed in your Word and in communion with you that those who see me know that I am yours and will believe that you are real. Help me to be one with you in my thoughts and words and actions.

༄

A PRAYER FOR TODAY

Lord Jesus, shape my attitudes and actions to
become one with you and the will of the Father.

The World Is Watching

The world was stunned by the grace and forgiveness of the families of Amish children who were shot in their school. In a similar way, the families of black parishioners shot in their church brought the same message to the world: in the name of Christ, love and forgiveness in spite of hatred and murder.

The evil powers constantly promote ethnic and religious division, sowing distorted doctrines and bitterness. But followers of Jesus who are determined to love as he loved bring a message of amazing grace from the God who so loved the world he sent his only Son.

We are to love as the Father loves Jesus and as Jesus loves the Father. We are to be one with them.

Yet what can that really mean—to be one with the holy God? The question stirs huge volumes of humility.

Theologians describing the Trinity emphasize the deference and love that Father, Son, and Holy Spirit give to each other. We are called to be full of deference and love for other believers . . . and to love our enemies . . . so that the world may see the good news is all about grace and redemption.

———— "Love Them as You Love Me" ————

SELECTIONS FROM JOHN 17

"I have given them the glory you gave me,
so they may be one as we are one.
I am in them and you are in me."

It's sobering, Lord, to see how hatred fuels so many of the world's troubles. Satan manipulates so ruthlessly! Protect me from his guiles and let me be one with you and one with the whole body of Christ.

Many Christians sing, "Praise God from whom all blessings flow," and I trust that my brothers and sisters in Christ have that same desire that I have. Let our unity with you be genuine. Form our beliefs from your truths so that your blessings flow.

"May they experience such perfect unity
that the world will know that you sent me
and that you love them as much as you love me."

Father in heaven, how could you possibly love me and other believers as much as you love your Son Jesus? These are things far too mysterious for me to fathom! Yet I bask in the wonder of it and rejoice in your redemption.

Help me to be one with all who believe in you. When I disagree with some of them, or feel threatened by some of them, help me to come to you in prayer. Help me to be one with all who love and serve you. Let the world see in me and those who call on your name evidence that we truly are one with "God who so loved the world."

A PRAYER FOR TODAY

As I hear about all the world's troubles this day, empower me to be an instrument of your peace and to bring blessings to others.

What Will We See?

Some fans pay thousands of dollars for a seat at the Super Bowl. Others will pay much more for a ride in space. Yet we don't have to spend thousands to see wonders. Try rising early one morning to watch the sun rise. You might see a brilliant magenta against black clouds. Or a sky full of cheerful peachy-pink and gray puffs. Or a canvas streaked with shades of plum that contrast sharply with the brilliant glow on the horizon. The wondrous sight will lift your spirit and soothe your soul.

An old woman once said her entrance into heaven would be like the sunrise, full of light and color and surprise.

Much has been written about the wonders of heaven. Yet here's the best thing: the greatest thing about it is not what's spectacular like a halftime show or fireworks filling the sky. The best thing about heaven is divine love.

That's what Jesus emphasized as he prayed the ultimate blessing for his followers . . .

———— "Your Love in Them" ————

SELECTIONS FROM JOHN 17

"Father, I want these whom you have given me
to be with me where I am.

Then they can see all the glory you gave me
because you loved me even before the world began!"

Many images come to my mind, Lord, when I think of heaven and your glory. When troubles surround me, it's good to think about the place you're preparing for us and what joys await.

Yet, Father in heaven, most of all help me to open my heart to your mercy and love. Help me to focus on what you desire me to dwell on this day as I continue my journey to your celestial home. Help me to see the needs of others around me and to respond as you would, so others can see more of your glory.

"O righteous Father,
the world doesn't know you,
but I do;
and these disciples know you sent me.
I have revealed you to them,
and I will continue to do so.
Then your love for me will be in them,
and I will be in them."

Lord, please continue to reveal yourself to me. Help me to follow your example by praying for others. Help me to listen for the whispers of your Spirit and to respond by the power of your Spirit to your love.

ᥫᩤ

A PRAYER FOR TODAY

Father, draw me into your dynamic love.
May your presence guide and equip me
and those I pray for throughout this day.

DAY 38

War in Heaven

As Jesus faced the ultimate crisis—with the culmination of the great war in heaven and the forces of good and evil converging on him—he told his disciples, "My soul is crushed with grief to the point of death."

What did he ask them to do? Only one thing: "Watch and pray."

Great drama is going on all over the world, and we wonder what it's really all about. We hear that "God is up to something" and the Bible assures us he is redeeming the world, yet we struggle with questions, apprehensions, and at times, sheer bewilderment.

How are we to live and to believe when so much is horrific and seems to refute God's love and care? What are we to do? What could ever prove to be *enough*? We are to watch and pray.

The disciples had only hints of what was going on as Jesus agonized in prayer at Gethsemane. We have hints of what God is up to, but we "see things imperfectly, like puzzling reflections in a mirror" and we are constantly surprised by what happens. The great dramas of the world continue, and what are we to do?

Watch and pray.

The Awful Hour

SELECTIONS FROM MARK 14

They went to the olive grove called Gethsemane,
and Jesus said, "Sit here while I go and pray."
He took Peter, James, and John with him,
and he became deeply troubled and distressed.
He told them,
"My soul is crushed with grief to the point of death.
Stay here and keep watch with me."

Lord, as the disciples knew little about what it cost you to secure our salvation or what was really going on that night, I know only fragments of truth about our world's spiritual warfare. Help me to watch and pray for your will to be done on earth, as it is in heaven.

He went on a little farther and fell to the ground.
He prayed that, if it were possible,
the awful hour awaiting him might pass him by.
"Abba, Father," he cried out, "everything is possible
     for you.
Please take this cup of suffering away from me.
Yet I want your will to be done, not mine."

It's stunning, Father, to consider how much your Son suffered here for us. Help us to pray in your Spirit with gratitude and faith.

There's so much suffering in this world, and we long for you to heal and cleanse and bring peace. I bring all of these troubles to you, Lord, including the suffering closest to me. Work in mighty ways as you have promised, as you worked through your Son, who accepted your will for earth's redemption. Thank you for the good news of the gospel.

Then he returned and found the disciples asleep.
He said to Peter, "Simon, are you asleep?
Couldn't you watch with me even one hour?
Keep watch and pray,
so that you will not give in to temptation."

Holy Spirit, keep me from sleeping through the critical hours when I should be listening to you. Help me to sense your presence and power. Wake me up, Lord, to what you are doing!

Let nothing be a temptation to me, but fill my mind and spirit with your grace and wonders.

༄

A PRAYER FOR TODAY

Whatever happens throughout this day,
Lord, help me to watch and pray and to trust
you and your redeeming love for the world.

DAY 39

Resurrection Joy

The book of Hebrews tells us Jesus endured the cross because of the joy awaiting him. Mary Magdalene and another Mary, after the angel told them Jesus had risen from the tomb, felt "great joy."

Jesus' joy becomes our joy . . .

Father, Son, and Holy Spirit share among them their unique and dynamic love and joy. The gospel of Luke tells us during his earthly ministry Jesus "was filled with the joy of the Holy Spirit." It's instructive that in Paul's listing of the fruits of the Spirit, love is the first fruit, and joy is the second.

The Bible, for all its stark depictions of the human condition, emphasizes joy. In the Psalms, in Isaiah and Jeremiah, in the Epistles, we're invited to "rejoice in the Lord," "praise him," and "shout for joy." We may seldom experience joy as euphoria, but we can choose joy daily by praising God and asking for his presence.

If we sense little joy, we might pray the words of Psalm 51: "Do not banish me from your presence, and don't take your Holy Spirit from me. Restore to me the joy of your salvation, and make me willing to obey you."

Sherwood Wirt in his acclaimed book *Jesus, Man of Joy* wrote, "What Jesus actually brought with Him from heaven was something more than a new start for humanity; it was a clear, bubbling, unpolluted delight in God and God's creation." Referring to Matthew 28:9 Wirt maintains that the usual translations of the word describing Jesus' resurrection greeting to the women don't adequately render the Greek word *chairete*. He describes its meaning as literally, "Oh joy!"

"Oh Joy!"

SELECTIONS FROM MATTHEW 28

Early on Sunday morning, as the new day was
dawning,
Mary Magdalene and the other Mary went out to
visit the tomb.
Suddenly there was a great earthquake!
For an angel of the Lord came down from heaven,
rolled aside the stone, and sat on it.
His face shone like lightning, and his clothing was
as white as snow. . . .
"Don't be afraid!" he said.

Sometimes, Lord, I do feel afraid when I realize how holy and full of glory you are in contrast to my sinfulness and self-centeredness. Thank you for your grace and promises of cleansing and forgiveness. Change my fears into gratitude and courage.

"I know you are looking for Jesus, who was crucified.
He isn't here! He is risen from the dead. . . .
The women . . . were very frightened but also filled
with great joy . . .
Jesus met them and greeted them. . . .
Then Jesus said to them, "Don't be afraid."

As I meditate on the resurrection, thank you, Lord, for the joy it continues to bring. As we affirm in our Easter celebrations, "He is risen . . . He is risen indeed!" Help me to share the joy and vibrant hope that your resurrection accomplished. When I feel fear, when joy is absent, help me to open my heart and mind to your thoughts and your promises and your victory over death and evil in this world.

⌒

A Prayer for Today

Lord, today I remember your resurrection
and all it has accomplished! Oh joy!

The Ultimate Answer to Prayer

As we read Jesus' stories in Luke 11—stories about giving bread to a persistent neighbor and giving good food rather than a scorpion or snake to a child—we come to Jesus' summation of their meaning: "If you sinful people know how to give good gifts to your children, how much more will your heavenly Father give the Holy Spirit to those who ask him."

Jesus invites us to ask for the presence of his Holy Spirit.

There's an intriguing link between Jesus' promise about the Holy Spirit and what happened after his resurrection. We see it fulfilled in the book of Acts when his followers were "constantly united in prayer." As they met together, "suddenly, there was a sound from heaven like the roaring of a mighty windstorm, and it filled the house where they were sitting. . . . And everyone present was filled with the Holy Spirit and began speaking in other languages, as the Holy Spirit gave them this ability."

Prayer . . . and then the coming of the Holy Spirit.

Peter, explaining to the crowd that gathered what was going on, quoted Joel's prophecy that God would pour out his Spirit. "God raised Jesus from the dead," Peter told them. "And the Father, as he had promised, gave him the Holy Spirit to pour out upon us, just as you see and hear today."

God's giving is connected with our asking. Jesus invites us to ask with trust and persistence for the presence of the Holy Spirit.

New Birth, New Life

SELECTIONS FROM TITUS 3

When God our Savior revealed his kindness and
love, he saved us,
not because of the righteous things we had done,
but because of his mercy.
He washed away our sins,
giving us a new birth and new life
through the Holy Spirit.

All praise to you, Lord, for your mercy and new life. I praise you that I can say no to sin because you live in me. May the Holy Spirit vitalize your life within me. Help me to live so that others will be drawn to your love and mercy.

He generously poured out the Spirit upon us
through Jesus Christ our Savior.
Because of his grace he made us right in his sight
and gave us confidence that we will inherit
eternal life.

Yes, you have been generous in pouring out your Spirit, Lord, and full of grace toward me and toward all those who have received your new life. Help us to keep in step with you and to be generous and full of grace as you are.

I want you to insist on these teachings
so that all who trust in God
will devote themselves to doing good.

Lord, in our troubled world, help us to trust in you and to devote ourselves to praying your will be done, and to "doing good" in every way we can, and to furthering your will on earth.

A Prayer for Today

Our Father in heaven, holy be your
name. Help me to live right now with
hope, joy, and love, sharing your mercy
and grace with my troubled world.

⌒∽

APPENDIX

Prayer throughout
the Scriptures

Discovering treasure—what an experience that would be! How would it feel to suddenly find hidden packets of cash or jewels buried in your back yard?

Jesus told the story of a man finding treasure in a field and selling all he had to own it. He was emphasizing the supreme value of spiritual treasure. He invites us to discover spiritual riches worthy of exuberance and full engagement.

Nick Harrison in his book *Magnificent Prayer* expresses amazement at what is offered. "Prayer is truly, wonderfully, amazingly *magnificent*. Prayer is an invitation to us from God Himself, asking us to please communicate with Him. Through prayer we speak to Almighty God and Almighty God speaks to us. Through prayer we ask for and receive good things from our heavenly Father. . . . Think of it—personal access to the most powerful and most loving Being in the universe."

In these forty days we've explored Jesus' intense focus on prayer, and we've prayed with the Scriptures' insights and challenges. Now I invite you to sample the spiritual wealth available to each of us in the full breadth of the Bible's wisdom about prayer.

Psalm 34 invites us to "taste and see that the LORD is good," even in our hardest, most troubled times.

The following selections comprise a smorgasbord of the Bible's stories, lessons, and impassioned, personal prayers. This appendix can be used in many ways. You can browse it for reminders of prayer's significance and ways you can deepen and enrich your prayer life. Maybe a verse will become your morning takeaway for the day ahead. You may want to journal your own prayers of response as we have during the past forty days.

To deepen your insights, you can go to the Bible chapters indicated to grasp the context for each portion—for instance, childless Hannah's passionate prayer, sinful David's desperate prayer, Daniel's fearless prayers, or Jonah's prayer in his day of terror.

Prayer in the context of trouble . . . praise in the joy of worship . . . prayer for forgiveness and grace . . . we can call on our Father in all circumstances, praying as the psalmist prayed:

Hear me as I pray, O LORD,
  Be merciful and answer me!
My heart has heard you say, "Come and talk with me."
  And my heart responds, "LORD, I am coming."

1. A Cry for Help

PSALM 5:1–3 NIV

Listen to my words, LORD,
  consider my lament.
Hear my cry for help,
  my King and my God,
  for to you I pray.

In the morning, LORD, you hear my voice;
  in the morning I lay my requests before you
  and wait expectantly.

2. Glorious Resources

EPHESIANS 3:14–18

When I think of all this, I fall to my knees and pray to the Father, the Creator of everything in heaven and on earth. I pray that from his glorious, unlimited resources he will empower you with inner strength through his Spirit. Then Christ will make his home in your hearts as you trust in him. Your roots will grow down into God's love and keep you strong. And may you have the power to understand, as all God's people should, how wide, how long, how high, and how deep his love is.

3. Bitter Prayer Answered

1 SAMUEL 1:10–17 NIV

In her deep anguish Hannah prayed to the LORD, weeping bitterly. And she made a vow, saying, "LORD Almighty, if you will only look on your servant's misery and remember me, and not forget your servant but give her a son, then I will give him to the LORD for all the days of his life, and no razor will ever be used on his head."

As she kept on praying to the LORD, Eli observed her mouth. Hannah was praying in her heart, and her lips were moving but her voice was not heard. Eli thought she was drunk and said to her, "How long are you going to stay drunk? Put away your wine."

"Not so, my lord," Hannah replied, "I am a woman who is deeply troubled. I have not been drinking wine or beer; I was pouring out my soul to the LORD. Do not take your servant for a wicked woman; I have been praying here out of my great anguish and grief."

Eli answered, "Go in peace, and may the God of Israel grant you what you have asked of him."

4. Jesus' All-Nighter

LUKE 6:12 ESV

In these days he went out to the mountain to pray, and all night he continued in prayer to God.

5. Sin, Guilt, Forgiveness

PSALM 32:3–7

When I refused to confess my sin,
    my body wasted away,
    and I groaned all day long.
Day and night your hand of discipline was heavy on me.
    My strength evaporated like water in the summer
        heat.
Finally, I confessed all my sins to you
    and stopped trying to hide my guilt.
I said to myself, "I will confess my rebellion to the LORD."
    And you forgave me! All my guilt is gone.

Therefore, let all the godly pray to you while there is
      still time,
    that they may not drown in the floodwaters of
      judgment.
For you are my hiding place;
    you protect me from trouble.
    You surround me with songs of victory.

6. Stunning Prayers for Us

ROMANS 8:26–27 NIV

In the same way, the Spirit helps us in our weakness. We do not know what we ought to pray for, but the Spirit himself intercedes for us through wordless groans. And he who searches our hearts knows the mind of the Spirit, because the Spirit intercedes for God's people in accordance with the will of God.

7. Bold Praying

DANIEL 6:6–11

So the administrators and high officers went to the king and said, "Long live King Darius! We are all in agreement—we administrators, officials, high officers, advisers, and governors—that the king should make a law that will be strictly enforced. Give orders that for the next thirty days any person who prays to anyone, divine or human—except to you, Your Majesty—will be thrown into the den of lions. And now, Your Majesty, issue and sign this law so it cannot be changed, an official law of the Medes and Persians that cannot be revoked." So King Darius signed the law.

But when Daniel learned that the law had been signed, he went home and knelt down as usual in his upstairs room, with its windows open toward Jerusalem. He prayed three times a day, just as he had always done, giving thanks to his God. Then the officials went together to Daniel's house and found him praying and asking for God's help.

8. Prayer as Priority

MATTHEW 14:22–23

Immediately after this, Jesus insisted that his disciples get back into the boat and cross to the other side of the lake, while he sent the people home. After sending them home, he went up into the hills by himself to pray. Night fell while he was there alone.

9. How to Pray for a Believer

COLOSSIANS 1:9–12 NIV

Since the day we heard about you, we have not stopped praying for you. We continually ask God to fill you with the knowledge of his will through all the wisdom and understanding that the Spirit gives, so that you may live a life worthy of the Lord and please him in every way: bearing fruit in every good work, growing in the knowledge of God, being strengthened with all power according to his glorious might so that you may have great endurance and patience, and giving joyful thanks to the Father, who has qualified you to share in the inheritance of his holy people in the kingdom of light.

10. Prayer When Threatened

NEHEMIAH 4:6–9

At last the wall was completed to half its height around the entire city, for the people had worked with enthusiasm.

But when Sanballat and Tobiah and the Arabs, Ammonites, and Ashdodites heard that the work was going ahead and that the gaps in the wall of Jerusalem were being repaired, they were furious. They all made plans to come and fight against Jerusalem and throw us into confusion. But we prayed to our God and guarded the city day and night to protect ourselves.

11. Pray for Peace

1 TIMOTHY 2:1–2

I urge you, first of all, to pray for all people. Ask God to help them; intercede on their behalf, and give thanks for them. Pray this way for kings and all who are in authority so that we can live peaceful and quiet lives marked by godliness and dignity.

12. Persistence

1 THESSALONIANS 5:16–17 ESV

Rejoice always, pray without ceasing.

13. Pray for the Holy Spirit

ACTS 8:14–15

When the apostles in Jerusalem heard that the people of Samaria had accepted God's message, they sent Peter and John there. As soon as they arrived, they prayed for these new believers to receive the Holy Spirit.

14. Attentive Ears in Heaven

2 CHRONICLES 7:12–15 ESV

Then the LORD appeared to Solomon in the night and said to him: "I have heard your prayer and have chosen this place for myself as a house of sacrifice. When I shut up the heavens so that there is no rain, or command the locust to devour the land, or send pestilence among my people, if my people who are called by my name humble themselves, and pray and seek my face and turn from their wicked ways, then I will hear from heaven and will forgive their sin and heal their land. Now my eyes will be open and my ears attentive to the prayer that is made in this place.

15. Warning: Get Clean
Isaiah 1:15–18

"When you lift up your hands in prayer, I will not look.
    Though you offer many prayers, I will not listen,
    for your hands are covered with the blood of
        innocent victims.
Wash yourselves and be clean!
    Get your sins out of my sight.
    Give up your evil ways.
Learn to do good.
    Seek justice.
Help the oppressed.
    Defend the cause of orphans.
    Fight for the rights of widows.

"Come now, let's settle this,"
    says the LORD.
"Though your sins are like scarlet,
    I will make them as white as snow.
Though they are red like crimson,
    I will make them as white as wool."

16. Love and Knowledge

PHILIPPIANS 1:9 NIV

And this is my prayer: that your love may abound more and more in knowledge and depth of insight.

17. Prayer, and Ready to Move

ROMANS 1:9–10

God knows how often I pray for you. Day and night I bring you and your needs in prayer to God, whom I serve with all my heart by spreading the Good News about his Son.

One of the things I always pray for is the opportunity, God willing, to come at last to see you.

18. The Hardest Prayers

LUKE 6:27–28 NIV

"But to you who are listening I say: Love your enemies, do good to those who hate you, bless those who curse you, pray for those who mistreat you."

19. Floods of Destruction

PSALM 18:3–6

I called on the LORD, who is worthy of praise,
    and he saved me from my enemies.

The ropes of death entangled me;
    floods of destruction swept over me.
The grave wrapped its ropes around me;
    death laid a trap in my path.

But in my distress I cried out to the LORD;
   yes, I prayed to my God for help.
He heard me from his sanctuary;
   my cry to him reached his ears.

20. Inspired Prayer for Others

EPHESIANS 1:15–20 NIV

For this reason, ever since I heard about your faith in the Lord Jesus and your love for all God's people, I have not stopped giving thanks for you, remembering you in my prayers. I keep asking that the God of our Lord Jesus Christ, the glorious Father, may give you the Spirit of wisdom and revelation, so that you may know him better. I pray that the eyes of your heart may be enlightened in order that you may know the hope to which he has called you, the riches of his glorious inheritance in his holy people, and his incomparably great power for us who believe. That power is the same as the mighty strength he exerted when he raised Christ from the dead and seated him at his right hand in the heavenly realms.

21. A Prayer of Desperation

JONAH 2:1–7 NIV

From inside the fish Jonah prayed to the LORD his God. He said:

"In my distress I called to the LORD,
   and he answered me.
From deep in the realm of the dead I called for help,
   and you listened to my cry.

You hurled me into the depths,
    into the very heart of the seas,
    and the currents swirled about me;
all your waves and breakers
    swept over me.
I said, 'I have been banished
    from your sight;
yet I will look again
    toward your holy temple.'
The engulfing waters threatened me,
    the deep surrounded me;
    seaweed was wrapped around my head.
To the roots of the mountains I sank down;
    the earth beneath barred me in forever.
But you, LORD my God,
    brought my life up from the pit.

"When my life was ebbing away,
    I remembered you, LORD,
and my prayer rose to you,
    to your holy temple."

22. God's Love and Freedom

PSALM 118:4–6 NIV

Let those who fear the LORD say:
    "His love endures forever."

When hard pressed, I cried to the LORD;
    he brought me into a spacious place.
The LORD is with me; I will not be afraid.
    What can mere mortals do to me?

23. Jesus: Pleading in Prayer

LUKE 22:31–32

"Simon, Simon, Satan has asked to sift each of you like wheat. But I have pleaded in prayer for you, Simon, that your faith should not fail. So when you have repented and turned to me again, strengthen your brothers."

24. Rough Times, Good Times

JAMES 5:13 NIV

Is anyone among you in trouble? Let them pray. Is anyone happy? Let them sing songs of praise.

25. Prayer and Restoration

JOB 42:10

When Job prayed for his friends, the LORD restored his fortunes. In fact, the LORD gave him twice as much as before!

26. Two Conditions of Prayer

COLOSSIANS 4:2 NIV

Devote yourselves to prayer, being watchful and thankful.

27. Freed From Fears

PSALM 34:1–8

I will praise the LORD at all times.
  I will constantly speak his praises.
I will boast only in the LORD;
  let all who are helpless take heart.

Come, let us tell of the LORD's greatness;
    let us exalt his name together.

I prayed to the LORD, and he answered me.
    He freed me from all my fears.
Those who look to him for help will be radiant
      with joy;
    no shadow of shame will darken their faces.
In my desperation I prayed, and the LORD listened;
    he saved me from all my troubles.
For the angel of the LORD is a guard;
    he surrounds and defends all who fear him.

Taste and see that the LORD is good.
    Oh, the joys of those who take refuge in him!

28. Prayer as Response to Jesus

REVELATION 3:20 NIV

"Here I am! I stand at the door and knock. If anyone hears my voice and opens the door, I will come in and eat with that person, and they with me."

29. Momentous Prayers

REVELATION 8:3–5 ESV

And another angel came and stood at the altar with a golden censer, and he was given much incense to offer with the prayers of all the saints on the golden altar before the throne, and the smoke of the incense, with the prayers of the saints, rose before God from the hand of the angel. Then the angel took the censer and filled it with fire from the altar and threw it on the earth, and there were peals

of thunder, rumblings, flashes of lightning, and an earthquake.

30. Peace of Mind

PHILIPPIANS 4:4–7 NIV

Rejoice in the Lord always. I will say it again: Rejoice!
Let your gentleness be evident to all. The Lord is near.
Do not be anxious about anything, but in every situation,
by prayer and petition, with thanksgiving, present your
requests to God. And the peace of God, which transcends
all understanding, will guard your hearts and your minds
in Christ Jesus.

NOTES

Day 2   **Oswald Chambers declared:** Oswald Chambers, *My Utmost for His Highest*, classic edition (© 1927, 1935, 1963; Grand Rapids: Discovery House, 2017), June 25 entry.

Day 8   **Eugene Peterson:** *The Message.* Copyright © by Eugene H. Peterson 1993, 1994, 1995, 1996, 2000, 2001, 2002. Used by permission of Tyndale House Publishers, Inc.

Day 11   **The well-respected book:** David Blankenhorn, *Fatherless America: Confronting Our Most Urgent Social Problem* (New York: HarperCollins, 1995).

Day 16   **A prolific author:** George MacDonald, *Unspoken Sermons: Series I, II, and III* (Jersey City, NJ: Start Publishing, 2012).

Day 17   **In *Journey of Prayer*:** Rosemary Budd, *Journey of Prayer* (London: Hodder & Stoughton, 1989).

Day 17   **MacDonald conveyed:** George MacDonald, *Unspoken Sermons: Series I, II, and III* (Jersey City, NJ: Start Publishing, 2012).

Day 18   ***Our Heavenly Father*:** Originally published in English as *The Prayer That Spans the World: Sermons on the Lord's Prayer*, by Helmut Thielicke (© 1953), trans. by John W. Doberstein (© 1965), Cambridge, UK: Lutterworth Press, 2016.

Day 22   **The prayer of St. Francis:** Alan Paton, *Instrument of Thy Peace: The Prayer of St. Francis*, 1968.

Day 29   **A. W. Tozer wrote:** A. W. Tozer, *The Knowledge of the Holy: Knowing God through His Attributes* (1961).

Day 32   **Philip Yancey once wrote:** Philip Yancey, *Prayer: Does It Make Any Difference* (Grand Rapids: Zondervan, 2006).

Day 39   **Sherwood Wirt:** Sherwood E. Wirt, *Jesus, Man of Joy*, Billy Graham Evangelistic Association edition, published with permission of Thomas Nelson.

Appendix **Nick Harrison:** Nick Harrison, *Magnificent Prayer* (Grand Rapids: Zondervan, 2001), 12–13.

Enjoy this book? Help us get the word out!

Share a link to the book or
mention it on social media

Write a review on your blog, on a retailer site,
or on our website (dhp.org)

Pick up another copy to share with someone

Recommend this book for your
church, book club, or small group

Follow Discovery House on
social media and join the discussion

Contact us to share your thoughts:

 @discoveryhouse    @DiscoveryHouse

Discovery House
P.O. Box 3566
Grand Rapids, MI 49501 USA

Phone: 1-800-653-8333
Email: books@dhp.org
Web: dhp.org